NONPROFIT EXECUTIVE COMPENSATION

PLANNING, PERFORMANCE, AND PAY

Second Edition

Brian Vogel and
Charles W. Quatt, Ph.D.

Library of Congress Cataloging-in-Publication Data

Vogel, Brian H.

  Nonprofit executive compensation : planning, performance, and pay / by
Brian Vogel and Charles W. Quatt. -- 2nd ed.

      p. cm. --

Rev. ed. of: Dollars and sense. c2005.

  Includes bibliographical references and index.

  ISBN 1-58686-117-4 (alk. paper)

1. Chief executive officers--Salaries, etc. 2. Nonprofit organizations--Management.
3. Compensation management. I. Quatt, Charles W. II. Vogel, Brian H. Dollars and
sense. III. Title.

          HD4965.2.V64 2009
          658.4'072--dc22   2009038968

© 2010 BoardSource.
First Printing, October 2009
ISBN 1-58686-117-4

Published by BoardSource
1828 L Street, NW, Suite 900
Washington, DC 20036

Building Effective Nonprofit Boards

BoardSource is dedicated to advancing the public good by building exceptional nonprofit boards and inspiring board service.

BoardSource was established in 1988 by the Association of Governing Boards of Universities and Colleges (AGB) and Independent Sector (IS). Prior to this, in the early 1980s, the two organizations had conducted a survey and found that although 30 percent of respondents believed they were doing a good job of board education and training, the rest of the respondents reported little, if any, activity in strengthening governance. As a result, AGB and IS proposed the creation of a new organization whose mission would be to increase the effectiveness of nonprofit boards.

With a lead grant from the Kellogg Foundation and funding from five other donors, BoardSource opened its doors in 1988 as the National Center for Nonprofit Boards with a staff of three and an operating budget of $385,000. On January 1, 2002, BoardSource took on its new name and identity. These changes were the culmination of an extensive process of understanding how we were perceived, what our audiences wanted, and how we could best meet the needs of nonprofit organizations.

Today, BoardSource is the premier voice of nonprofit governance. Its highly acclaimed products, programs, and services mobilize boards so that organizations fulfill their missions, achieve their goals, increase their impact, and extend their influence. BoardSource is a 501(c)(3) organization.

BoardSource provides

- resources to nonprofit leaders through workshops, training, and an extensive Web site (www.boardsource.org)

- governance consultants who work directly with nonprofit leaders to design specialized solutions to meet an organization's needs

- the world's largest, most comprehensive selection of material on nonprofit governance, including a large selection of books and CD-ROMs

- an annual conference that brings together approximately 900 governance experts, board members, and chief executives and senior staff from around the world

For more information, please visit our Web site at www.boardsource.org, e-mail us at mail@boardsource.org, or call us at 800-883-6262.

Have You Used These BoardSource Resources?

THE GOVERNANCE SERIES

1. *Ten Basic Responsibilities of Nonprofit Boards, Second Edition*
2. *Legal Responsibilities of Nonprofit Boards, Second Edition*
3. *Financial Responsibilities of Nonprofit Boards, Second Edition*
4. *Fundraising Responsibilities of Nonprofit Boards, Second Edition*
5. *The Nonprofit Board's Role in Mission, Planning, and Evaluation, Second Edition*
6. *Structures and Practices of Nonprofit Boards, Second Edition*

BOOKS

Chief Executive Transitions: How to Hire and Support a Nonprofit CEO

Chief Executive Succession Planning: The Board's Role in Securing Your Organization's Future

Assessment of the Chief Executive

Understanding Nonprofit Financial Statements, Third Edition

The Nonprofit Board Answer Book: A Practical Guide for Board Members and Chief Executives, Second Edition

Navigating the Organizational Lifecycle: A Capacity-Building Guide for Nonprofit Leaders

Financial Committees

The Nonprofit Policy Sampler, Second Edition

The Board Chair Handbook, Second Edition

Getting the Best from Your Board: An Executive's Guide to a Successful Partnership

Taming the Troublesome Board Member

The Board Building Cycle: Nine Steps to Finding, Recruiting, and Engaging Nonprofit Board Members, Second Edition

The Nonprofit Dashboard: A Tool for Tracking Progress

The Nonprofit Legal Landscape

The Nonprofit Board's Guide to Bylaws

Managing Conflicts of Interest: A Primer for Nonprofit Boards, Second Edition

Moving Beyond Founder's Syndrome to Nonprofit Success

The Source: Twelve Principles of Governance That Power Exceptional Boards

Exceptional Board Practices: The Source in Action

Fearless Fundraising for Nonprofit Boards, Second Edition

Driving Strategic Planning: A Nonprofit Executive's Guide

Culture of Inquiry: Healthy Debate in the Boardroom

Who's Minding the Money?: An Investment Guide for Nonprofit Board Members, Second Edition

DVDs

Meeting the Challenge: An Orientation to Nonprofit Board Service

Speaking of Money: A Guide to Fundraising for Nonprofit Board Members

ONLINE ASSESSMENTS

Board Self-Assessment

Assessment of the Chief Executive

Executive Search — Needs Assessment

For an up-to-date list of publications and information about current prices, membership, and other services, please call BoardSource at 800-883-6262 or visit our Web site at www.boardsource.org. For consulting services, please e-mail us at consulting@boardsource.org or call 877-892-6293.

CONTENTS

ACKNOWLEDGMENTS

For this second edition of *Nonprofit Executive Compensation: Planning, Performance, and Pay,* (previously titled *Dollars and Sense*) the authors again thank first our original staff partners at BoardSource — Marla Bobowick, who first suggested to Charlie Quatt that we write a piece on chief executive compensation; Claire Perella, who managed the writing and editing process; and our editor Deborah Kennedy. For the second edition, we add our new partners: our editor, Danielle Henry, and Karen Hansen, BoardSource's director of publications.

We again thank Celia Roady and Greg Needles of Morgan, Lewis & Bockius for their help in understanding the complicated legal regime that applies to nonprofit chief executive compensation. Without Celia's unsurpassed knowledge of nonprofit law — not to mention her editing skills, and Greg's expertise on deferred compensation —we never would have been able to complete the legal sections of the book.

For their work on the first draft, thanks remain due to two former members of Quatt Associates: Alex Rabinovich for his meticulous review and editing of multiple drafts, and to both Alex and Chris Potter for their research assistance.

For the second draft, we have had the invaluable support of our Quatt Associates colleague Thomas Schumann, who deserves to be considered the third author of this edition. Reid Thompson, also a colleague at Quatt, was our source on the IRS Form 990.

To everyone who helped us, your assistance was invaluable; any remaining faults are ours.

INTRODUCTION

Hiring and retaining the chief executive are among the most important functions of a nonprofit organization's board. While the board is ultimately responsible for the organization's mission and strategy, the chief executive is the executor — and very often the main architect — of that strategy.

Recruiting and retaining the best possible chief executive often depends on offering the right compensation plan. An effective compensation plan enables a board to hire the best candidate for the job. The plan then provides feedback on performance and helps retain a good chief executive by rewarding effective leadership of the organization.

In developing the chief executive compensation plan, the board must execute a careful balancing act. On the one hand, it must offer a strong salary and benefits package in order to attract the best possible candidates for the chief executive position, and to keep that person in office. On the other hand, it must not offer a compensation package that is out of line with the organization's mission or with the overall culture of the nonprofit sector, whose work is regarded, both within and outside the sector, as properly being driven by mission rather than profit.

INCREASED PUBLIC AND IRS SCRUTINY

To complicate matters, the environment in which boards must make decisions about chief executive compensation has become more difficult. Outside scrutiny of nonprofit salaries has increased; both the media and the Internal Revenue Service (IRS) are paying much closer attention than they have in the past to nonprofit, and especially chief executive, compensation. In June 2004, the IRS announced that it was stepping up scrutiny of nonprofit salaries and hiring 73 new auditors to review compensation for executives at nonprofit organizations for compliance with IRS regulations.[1] In March 2007, the IRS reported on the initial results of its investigation. While it did not find major compliance problems, 30 percent of the more than 1,200 organizations examined had to amend their IRS Form 990 tax returns, and the IRS assessed more than $21 million in proposed excise taxes.[2] In April 2009, the IRS director of tax-exempt organizations "warned nonprofits to be mindful of executive compensation practices" and again announced additions to IRS

---

[1] Elizabeth Schwinn, "Big Nonprofit Salaries Face Government Scrutiny," *Chronicle of Philanthropy*, June 24, 2004; Joann Lublin, "Compensation at Nonprofits Is Scrutinized Amid Lawsuits," *Wall Street Journal* Online, June 1, 2004, www.careerjournal.com/salaryhiring/industries/nonprofits/20040601-lublin.html.

[2] Internal Revenue Service, Report on *Exempt Organizations Executive Compensation Compliance Project—Parts I and II*. March 2007, www.irs.gov/pub/irs-tege/exec._comp._final.pdf.

audit staff.[3] The IRS continues to face pressure from Congress to review nonprofit compensation some lawmakers view as "excessive."[4]

In addition, changes to the information that must be reported on the IRS Form 990, effective beginning in the 2008 tax year, are likely to increase scrutiny of nonprofit compensation practices. The new 990 will mandate much more detailed disclosure of chief executive compensation, as well as the compensation for other senior and highly compensated nonprofit executives.[5]

IRS FORM 990

Most nonprofit organizations with annual budgets over $25,000 are required to file an IRS Form 990 or 990-EZ every year (see the instructions to the most recent IRS Form 990 for exceptions; private foundations file a 990-PF form). Form 990 data are available to the public; the Form 990s from the past three years must be made available to anyone who visits a nonprofit and asks for them, and nonprofits have 30 days to send out a photocopy if one is requested in writing. If an organization posts its Form 990 on the Internet, however, it is exempt from the other disclosure requirements. The nonprofit organization GuideStar (www.guidestar.org), posts approximately 4.6 million Form 990s on the Web. Other organizations, including the *Chronicle of Philanthropy,* also publish selected Form 990 data from time to time.

As of the 2008 tax year, the IRS Form 990 (but not the 990-PF) will require nonprofits to report compensation for all officers, directors, trustees and "key employees" (persons making over $150,000 a year in taxable compensation, having substantial influence over the organization, and among the top 20 highest paid employees). Organizations must break out compensation in more detail than in the past, report on perquisites, and describe their process for establishing the compensation of the chief executive.

See Appendix I for more on the new IRS Form 990.

State regulators, too, are cracking down on potentially excessive chief executive compensation; state attorneys general are bringing lawsuits that result in judgments ordering chief executives to repay millions of dollars in excess compensation. California's adoption of the California Nonprofit Integrity Act of 2004, which took effect in January 2005, requires the boards of charitable organizations with revenues of at least $2 million to review and approve the chief executive's compensation package to ensure its reasonableness. More and more state legislatures are on the road to tightening regulation of the internal practices of nonprofits — with compensation becoming increasingly important. State attorneys general — in

[3] Mike Spector, "IRS Probes Nonprofit Pay Practices," *Wall Street Journal,* April 6, 2009, http://online.wsj.com/article/SB123902531992992777.html.

[4] Lisa Wangsness, "Nonprofit Hospitals Targeted on Leader Pay," *Boston Globe,* March 4, 2009, www.boston.com/news/health/articles/2009/03/04/nonprofit_hospitals_targeted_on_leader_pay/. See also Planned Giving Design Center, "Grassley Calls on IRS to Review Problems in Tax-Exempt Arena," June 1, 2006, www.pgdc.com/pgdc/news-story/2006/06/02/grassley-calls-irs-review-problems-tax-exempt-arena.

[5] Internal Revenue Service, *Instructions for Form 990 2008,* pp. 1–2, 20–27, www.irs.gov/pub/irs-pdf/i990.pdf.

California, New York, Texas and elsewhere — are aggressively pursuing nonprofits perceived as overcompensating their chief executives (and other senior staff).

A series of high-profile cases have attracted press scrutiny that has seriously affected the reputation of leading nonprofit organizations, including arts organizations, foundations, and universities — and destroying, in some cases, the careers of their chief executives. One recent example involved the Museum of Modern Art. The *New York Times* reported in 2007 that a trust created by several of the Museum's board members had been covering the director's housing costs. This was not reported to the IRS as compensation. In other cases, the former president of American University and the former secretary of the Smithsonian came under scrutiny for charging allegedly lavish and unnecessary business expenses, and were forced to resign.[6]

As a consequence of this scrutiny, many nonprofits have made commendable progress in changing their compensation plans and increasing the transparency of their processes for setting compensation and reviewing chief executive performance on a regular basis. Sound practices are not, however, universal. Many boards still do not take full steps to monitor chief executive compensation. BoardSource, for example, found that only 67 percent of full boards approve the chief executive's compensation.[7] While, as we discuss in more detail later (see pages 12–13), there is no federal legal requirement that the full board formally approve chief executive compensation, the full board needs to know what it is paying, and therefore we strongly recommend that the full board in fact review and approve chief executive compensation. The new IRS Form 990 asks if the board has received and understood the form, with its detailed compensation information, before the form is finalized and filed.[8] This is an unsubtle hint in favor of full board review.

TRENDS IN CHIEF EXECUTIVE COMPENSATION

Perhaps not coincidentally, the increased scrutiny from the government, the press, and the public comes at a time when compensation practices at many nonprofits are coming to resemble, at least to some degree, those in the for-profit sector. Salaries at many nonprofits have been rising, and salaries at some large nonprofits have reached levels formerly associated only with parts of the for-profit marketplace.[9] In addition, some nonprofits have introduced compensation features such as bonuses, incentives, and deferred compensation that were formerly seen almost exclusively among for-profit corporations. Some nonprofits have found that these compensation features can offer distinct advantages in encouraging focused performance while controlling

[6] Stephanie Strom, "Donors Sweetened Director's Pay at MoMA," *New York Times* Online, February 16, 2007, www.nytimes.com/2007/02/16/arts/design/16moma.html?ex=1329282000&en=f0af57672ca3cadf&ei=5090&partner=rssuserland&emc=rss; Susan Kinzie and Valerie Strauss, "Trustees Oust AU's Ladner as President," Washington Post Online, October 11, 2005, www.washingtonpost.com/wp-dyn/content/article/2005/10/10/AR2005101000808.html.

[7] BoardSource, *Nonprofit Governance Index 2007,* p. 18.

[8] Internal Revenue Service, *Instructions for Form 990 2008,* p. 15.

[9] Noelle Barton and Ben Gose, "Executive Pay Outpaces Inflation: Median Compensation Rose 5 percent," *Chronicle of Philanthropy,* October 2, 2008.

compensation costs — although, as we discuss in more detail later in the book, they are not for everyone. The IRS has recognized that untraditional forms of compensation, such as bonuses and incentives, can contribute to stronger and more successful nonprofit organizations. Estimates of the percentage of nonprofits with chief executive bonus or incentive programs vary: A 2008 Quatt Associates survey of large nonprofit organizations showed that 62.5 percent offered such programs. The same survey found that 20 percent of chief executives of major foundations received incentives (a 2007 survey by the Council on Foundations found that 24 percent of foundations offered incentive pay to chief executives). A Quatt survey of academic institutions found that 23 percent of chief executives received incentives, while a 2008–2009 survey by the College and University Personnel Association found that bonuses were paid to 11.8 percent of chief executives of single institutions and 2.6 percent of chief executives of multiple-institution systems.[10]

Of course, few nonprofit organizations have the luxury of offering excessive compensation to any of their staff members; the challenge that many smaller organizations face is not to control unreasonably high salaries, but to find enough money to pay reasonable salaries at all. This all-too-common financial challenge is one of the reasons that chief executive compensation in the nonprofit sector, like sector salaries in general, remains below the levels found in the for-profit world. In addition, nonprofits cannot offer some of the more lucrative features found in for-profit compensation, such as equity, and deferred compensation in the nonprofit sector is subject to stricter rules than it is in the for-profit world.

Q **What are the trends toward making nonprofit salaries competitive?**

A Nonprofit salaries rose steadily through 2008, and at least among larger and more complex nonprofits, the gap in salary compensation between for-profits and nonprofits narrowed. Moreover, some pay practices, such as bonus and deferred compensation, formerly seen only in for-profit organizations, have become increasingly common in nonprofit organizations.

That said, nonprofit total compensation still lags behind for-profit pay for positions of the same impact and complexity, and probably always will. In part this is because nonprofits cannot offer equity or other lucrative forms of long-term compensation. The larger reason, however, is that external scrutiny, federal and state oversight, and the internal culture of nonprofits generally discourage the payment of very high levels of compensation. For many nonprofits, financial considerations are also significant limits on executive pay.

The bottom line: Many nonprofits are now appropriately competitive — paying enough to ensure they can hire the talent they need, but not so much that they risk violating the public trust that expects them to focus on their main responsibility, their mission.

---

[10] Quatt Associates, *2008 Not-for-Profit Compensation Survey,* p. 10; Council on Foundations, *2007 Grantmakers Salary and Benefits Report,* p. 51; Quatt Associates, *2006 Proprietary Survey of Compensation at Academic Institutions,* p. 6; College and University Personnel Association, *Administrative Compensation Survey for the 2008-09 Academic Year,* p. 11.

PUBLIC EXPECTATIONS

Perhaps the most significant factor differentiating compensation for chief executives in the nonprofit sector from that of their counterparts in for-profit businesses is public expectation. The public rightly believes that a nonprofit organization has a responsibility to channel as much of its donor money as possible toward the fulfillment of its mission. Many members of the public also believe that staff at nonprofits should be willing to receive lower salaries than staff members in comparable positions in for-profit businesses, because the nonprofit staff person is dedicated to the organization's mission.[11] These expectations create a value system in which an apparently generous, and perhaps appropriate, salary is seen to imply a lack of dedication to the organization and its mission. Compensation practices that are universal in the for-profit sector, and increasingly common among nonprofits, such as pay for performance and bonuses, are sometimes perceived as inappropriate.

Nonprofit boards must be prepared to work within the constraints imposed by this publicly held value system. They must also recognize that the same value system may be an integral part of their organization's internal culture as well. When this is the case, board members and staff alike may object to the use of market-based comparisons for making salary determinations and to the provision of benefits and perquisites for the chief executive. They may even resist giving the chief executive more than a token annual salary increase.

Q Are chief executive pay records public information? What about the pay of other employees?

A Chief executive pay, including cash pay and benefits, must be reported on the annual IRS Form 990 that almost all tax-exempt organizations must file. Organizations must also report on their 990s compensation for: a) officers, directors, and trustees; b) "key employees" (the top 20 employees who receive at least $150,000 in reportable income and have fiscal or program management responsibility for at least 10 percent of the organization's financial resources); and c) the top five employees not included in (a) or (b) who receive at least $100,000 in reportable compensation. IRS Form 990s must be made available to the public upon request.

BALANCING PUBLIC EXPECTATIONS WITH THE NEED TO COMPETE FOR STRONG LEADERSHIP

On the other hand, boards need to be aware that unrealistically low expectations about executive compensation can be detrimental to a nonprofit organization. The chief executive is a nonprofit's single-most-important employee. Failure to pay a competitive salary, however noble the motivation for doing so, can cause a nonprofit

---

[11] Sarah Z. Sleeper, "Sizing Up San Diego's Nonprofit CEO Pay," *San Diego Metropolitan,* June 2004; Negative public perception may lead to a loss of funding sources — in May of 2009, a Maryland county withdrew $55,000 in grants to a public charity to protest what it believed was excessive pay for the charity's CEO, "MontCo Withholds Money to Charity Because of High Executive Pay," *Washington Examiner,* May 12, 2009.

to lose a strong chief executive or find it almost impossible to recruit an effective one, harming the organization's success and its ability to fulfill its mission. Below-market chief executive compensation can also act as a cap on the pay of other senior staff, leading to further losses in effectiveness as key employees are recruited away by other organizations.

Board members should therefore consider very carefully the potential costs of underpaying their organization's chief executive. Competitive salaries, based on the nonprofit marketplace, and innovative compensation practices — for organizations that can afford them and are prepared to justify them — can help recruit and retain skilled and experienced leaders. For organizations that are facing budget constraints, it may make sense to economize in other areas rather than risk the loss of an effective organizational leader. Of course, each nonprofit must decide for itself what mix of compensation features makes the most sense for its circumstances.

A nonprofit organization's board can most effectively meet public expectations and justify its decisions regarding chief executive compensation when it approaches compensation as a strategic decision. The board's principal duty in setting chief executive pay, in addition to meeting legal norms and stakeholder expectations, is to ensure that the compensation package supports organizational success. The compensation package must be an integral part of overall organizational strategy and planning. By ensuring that the chief executive's compensation will contribute to the realization of the organization's mission and objectives, the board provides a rationale for its decisions that will stand up to public scrutiny.

As we were completing the second edition of this book, a severe economic downturn was affecting nonprofit and for-profit compensation alike. After a long run of good years, nonprofits face falling budgets, hiring freezes or layoffs, and even the prospect of having to sharply cut back or cease their operations. The long-term effect on nonprofit compensation is unpredictable, although a slowdown in rising compensation levels seems likely. However, difficult economic times may also make it even more important to recruit and retain the best possible talent in a way that respects public concerns and perceptions.

WHAT YOU WILL FIND IN THIS BOOK

This book is intended as a practical guide for nonprofit boards to use in setting chief executive compensation — both when hiring a new leader and when reviewing the pay of a sitting chief executive. It is designed to serve as a reference tool and as a step-by-step guide that a board can use to establish an effective compensation structure within the context of the organization's mission, history, goals, and marketplace. It seeks to provide information and guidelines that will be useful to nonprofits of all sizes, while recognizing that small, medium-sized, and large nonprofits have differing needs and circumstances. Above all, it aims to help nonprofits of all types increase the transparency and integrity of their chief executive compensation practices as part of their stewardship of the public trust.

Chapter 1 discusses the board's role in setting chief executive compensation. It places the issue in the larger context of the board's responsibilities to the organization, and outlines procedures for the board to follow in setting chief executive compensation. Chapter 2 covers the role of organizational culture, mission, and strategy in setting chief executive compensation. Chapter 3 explains how to develop a profile of the specific qualities desired in the chief executive. A formal profile helps a board target its recruitment to the correct marketplace and set compensation in light of the marketplace and desired skills; it is also helpful in determining how to reward those skills. Chapter 4 discusses the compensation philosophy: the set of values and mechanisms used to set compensation. Chapter 5 describes how to define the chief executive's marketplace and obtain data from the marketplace for use in setting compensation. Chapter 6 focuses on the legal requirements surrounding chief executive compensation, and how the board should act to protect itself, and the organization's executives, from liability. Chapter 7 discusses disclosure and explanation of chief executive compensation to the organization's various stakeholders, including staff, donors, and the public. Chapter 8 discusses the elements of the compensation package and their implementation. Chapter 9 covers chief executive employment agreements.

Readers familiar with the previous edition will find the following updates and additions:

- Impact of the new 990, and how to use the new data it will provide

- Additional guidance on how to use survey data in market pricing

- Sample compensation committee charter

- Expanded section on legal standards

- Sample chief executive job description

- Guidance on setting and adjusting compensation in difficult economic times

- The board's role in reviewing compensation for other senior executives beyond the chief executive

USING THIS BOOK

This book is organized to provide a logical, step-by-step method for boards to follow in thinking about chief executive compensation. We understand, however, that concepts referenced in one section may raise questions that are answered in detail only in subsequent sections. We have therefore included answers to frequently asked questions (FAQs) throughout the text. A full list of these FAQs is also included as Appendix II. We have also included boxes on major subjects and concepts for ease of reference.

CHAPTER 1

UNDERSTANDING THE BOARD'S ROLE IN SETTING CHIEF EXECUTIVE COMPENSATION

In one sense, the board's role in setting chief executive compensation is simple: The board is responsible for recruiting and hiring the chief executive, overseeing the chief executive's performance, and, if necessary, firing him or her. Setting the chief executive's compensation is also part of this responsibility.

However, the board's responsibility is more complex than this simple statement would suggest. The board must not only create a compensation plan that will be an effective tool both in recruitment and in performance evaluation — it must also set compensation in light of its responsibilities to the organization.

- **Mission responsibility:** The board ensures that the organization will achieve its mission through its oversight of the organization's long-term strategy and objectives. This means that the board must hire a chief executive who will be effective in implementing that strategy, leading the organization toward mission achievement. The compensation structure is an essential element of the board's ability to attract such a chief executive. However, the compensation structure itself must also *reinforce* the organization's strategy. A strategic compensation structure will reward success and send the appropriate signals if performance falls short; it will work best if it is part of an overall performance management plan tied to board-approved annual and long-term goals and objectives.

- **Fiduciary responsibility:** The board has a duty to maintain the organization's financial integrity. The board must strike a balance that allows it to hire the best possible chief executive without breaking the bank.

As Dennis Pointer and James Orlikoff suggest in *The High Performance Board* (San Francisco: Jossey-Bass, 2002, p. 37), "CEO compensation should be viewed as an important investment in the organization's future, not an expense. Value added to the organization by the CEO should be a huge multiple of total compensation. Your board must be prudent, but not penny wise and pound foolish."

Paying too low a salary can result in difficulty recruiting and retaining an effective leader, to the detriment of managerial decision making and ultimately of the organization's overall effectiveness. A salary that is too low can also depress salaries throughout the organization. A chief executive's salary that is so low that it limits salaries for other positions to levels that are not market-competitive impairs an organization's ability to hire and retain qualified and effective candidates for those positions.

Paying too high a salary, on the other hand, can create mistrust among stakeholders, incur public disapproval, and potentially subject the organization to legal and press scrutiny.

- **Legal and public responsibility:** The board must ensure that the organization complies with legal standards and meets the test of public and stakeholder scrutiny. This is not just an ethical responsibility. The IRS's intermediate sanctions regulations, which are explained in detail in Chapter 6, require that compensation for certain high-ranking individuals at most 501(c)(3) and 501(c)(4) organizations, including chief executives, not exceed an amount defined as reasonable by the regulations' standards. Board members who knowingly participate in the approval of compensation found to violate the standards are subject to *personal* liability and a fine of up to $20,000. Executives who receive excessive compensation are subject to even more severe penalties.

Q Which laws should the board be familiar with when setting the chief executive's compensation?

A Board members need to be familiar with the IRS intermediate sanctions rules and related legal doctrines, such as the private inurement doctrine. They also need to understand the state law applying to their nonprofit. If the board considers deferred compensation arrangements, it needs to understand the federal tax law governing such arrangements. See our discussion of legal issues in Chapters 6 and 8.

Q What is a legal cap on executive compensation?

A The legal cap, as laid out in the intermediate sanctions rules and related legal doctrines, is that "excess" compensation cannot be paid — i.e., more than is justified by the benefit the executive brings to the organization and by the compensation practices of "like organizations" in the marketplace. Chapter 6 in this book explains in detail how to determine excessive compensation under intermediate sanctions.

ESTABLISH A PROCEDURE

In order to fulfill its duties in these three areas of responsibility, the board needs to establish a procedure for determining chief executive compensation before it begins the recruiting and hiring process or the review for a current chief executive. This procedure should be formally outlined in writing for future reference.

The board should begin by determining its internal structure for overseeing chief executive compensation. That structure may take one of three forms.

1. *Compensation Committee or Task Force.* Where the board is too large and unwieldy to manage the compensation process as a group, it may delegate oversight of chief executive compensation to a special compensation committee or task force. A smaller committee can devote its attention as needed to the often-detailed process of managing compensation matters. Over time, committee members can also develop experience and expertise in this area. In

many organizations, the compensation committee also reviews the senior staff compensation levels suggested by the chief executive (especially those subject to the intermediate sanctions regulations), and it can take the lead in setting annual performance objectives and reviewing chief executive and organizational performance. A sample compensation committee charter can be found in Appendix III.

2. *Executive Committee.* If the board wishes to delegate compensation matters to a smaller committee but does not have the desire or personnel to form a separate compensation committee, chief executive and staff compensation may be handled by the board's executive committee.

3. *Whole Board.* In small and medium-sized nonprofits and in nonprofits with small boards, oversight of chief executive compensation may be handled by the board as a whole.

For the sake of simplicity, the remainder of this book will refer to the compensation committee as taking the lead in managing the chief executive compensation process. This implies no judgment as to the appropriate structure for any particular board. As we use it here, the term "compensation committee" applies to any board group that is managing the process.

Q **Should the entire board be aware of and/or approve the chief executive's salary and benefits each year?**

A We strongly recommend that the entire board review and approve the chief executive's salary and benefits. The board may delegate responsibility for producing recommendations and the data to back them up to a smaller group or committee of board members. However, the final compensation package should be approved by the board as a whole. There is one caveat: Only independent board members (i.e., those whose compensation or employment are not subject to the chief executive, or stand to otherwise benefit from approving the chief executive's compensation) should be involved in the final approval process.

There are several reasons why it is imperative for the full board to review and approve the final compensation package. The board should be comfortable that the compensation package complies with the intermediate sanctions regulations. Nonprofit chief executive compensation is also public information which must be reported on the organization's IRS Form 990. All board members should consider the public scrutiny that may be generated by the compensation package, and fully prepared to justify the package. There is now an additional reason for the board to consider public reaction to the decision on chief executive compensation: The new IRS Form 990 asks whether the Form 990 has been shared with the board. A board that does not review the 990 (including the chief executive compensation, which must appear on it) may face questions about the effectiveness of the organization's governance process.

Review and final approval of chief executive compensation by the full board (regardless of whether or not a separate committee is responsible for the major responsibilities involving compensation) is, as we have noted, something we strongly recommend as good practice. In fact, we consider it vital because chief executive compensation is public domain information. It is disappointing, therefore, that according to BoardSource's *Nonprofit Governance Index 2007*, only 67 percent of full boards approve the chief executive's total compensation package.[12] Each board member should understand and be able to justify the full board's compensation decision, as well as the board's overall process for setting and reviewing chief executive compensation, including the respective roles of the full board and any smaller committee(s).

As board members seek to determine which internal structure (the full board, or a compensation committee) will work best for their organization, the answers to these questions may provide guidance:

1. Is our board small and efficient enough to handle chief executive compensation matters as a group? Would the two-step process of committee work followed by full board review be more cumbersome for us than full board discussion of these matters?

2. Do we currently have access to the expertise we need to make informed decisions, either among our board members or with outside resources (legal advisor, compensation consultant, accountant, board members from other organizations)?

3. Are we more comfortable with assigning oversight of chief executive compensation to our executive committee, or to a separate compensation committee?

4. Do we have board members who are willing and able to take the lead as part of a compensation committee, executive committee, or special task force?

Once the board has decided on the appropriate structure for managing compensation, it then needs to consider and approve the subsequent steps in its overall procedure for establishing chief executive compensation. It is the responsibility of the board chair to coordinate the process and to ensure that the appropriate board members and committees fulfill their roles in the process. This includes the review of compensation for intermediate sanctions purposes (see discussion on pages 64–65).

The committee must exclude any person with a conflict of interest (that is, anyone whose employment is subject to the person whose compensation he or she would approve, or anyone who would otherwise stand to benefit financially from approving the compensation).[13] A formal, structured review of compensation by the board is especially important; it establishes a "rebuttable presumption of reasonableness," which shifts the burden of proving that compensation is excessive to the IRS; it also

[12] BoardSource, *Nonprofit Governance Index 2007*, p. 18.

[13] Bruce Hopkins, *The Law of Intermediate Sanctions*, (New York: John Wiley & Sons, 2003), pp. 164–165.

exempts board members from personal liability if certain procedures are followed (see Chapter 6).

Although the tasks in setting compensation are outlined in a sequential way here and in the chapters that follow, the overall process is not a linear one. The compensation committee will need to start with some sense of the possibilities and constraints that its mission, goals, and budget dictate for salary, benefits, and other compensation, and use those as reference points throughout the study and research process. Completion of each of the tasks outlined here will help the committee develop a realistic and effective compensation plan.

The board should also review its governance procedures and structure regularly, and make changes as necessary to ensure its continuing effectiveness and compliance with legal standards.

CHECKLIST FOR ESTABLISHING A CHIEF EXECUTIVE COMPENSATION PLAN

____ Ensure that board has complete information on current compensation (see this chapter, below).

____ Ensure that the chief executive compensation plan supports the organization's mission, goals, and strategy (Chapter 2).

____ Establish the chief executive job description and profile (and title, if necessary) (Chapter 3).

____ Develop the organization's compensation philosophy (Chapter 4).

____ Understand the marketplace; acquire and analyze appropriate market data on compensation practices in comparable organizations (Chapter 5).

____ Ensure that the compensation level and structure will meet legal requirements; establish a process for documenting the chief executive compensation decision and ensure that the process is followed; retain legal counsel if necessary (Chapter 6).

____ Review compensation for purposes of stakeholder and public scrutiny (Chapter 7).

____ Establish the compensation level and plan (Chapter 8).

____ Establish an ongoing process for reviewing chief executive compensation and job performance. The process should include setting annual and long-term goals, conducting annual performance reviews, and adjusting compensation each year based on market and performance (Chapter 8).

____ Identify negotiation points with respect to the chief executive contract (Chapter 9).

____ Ensure the compensation of other disqualified persons is reasonable and consistent with the organization's mission and purpose (see Chapter 6, box on page 72).

It is essential that the compensation committee start with accurate, detailed, and *complete* information about the current compensation packages for the chief executive and other senior staff. Particularly in situations where the full board has not previously been involved in setting chief executive compensation, full disclosure of the base pay level, the types and amounts of bonuses, and all benefits, as well as the rationale for each, is crucial (several prominent nonprofits have been embarrassed in recent years when chief executive perquisites not revealed to the full board became public knowledge). Organization staff must provide complete and detailed compensation information when the board requests it; typically, the board establishes a formal reporting mechanism through which the staff provides compensation information to the board chair, the chair of the compensation committee, or the compensation committee as a whole.

Q Our board has not historically approved the chief executive's salary and benefit package. We currently do not know specifics, so we need to get that information. Is it acceptable to ask the chief executive to give us his salary, cost of health insurance, pension, and other information?

A It is not just acceptable, it is essential that you know your chief executive's compensation. There should be a formal board process for receiving information about executive compensation, and with today's legal and public scrutiny, compensation information is best shared with the entire board. The board, either in its entirety or through a delegated committee, is responsible for setting chief executive pay. We strongly recommend that the full board make the final decision on pay; it is strongly encouraged by the IRS to review compensation in detail. The board cannot do its job without knowing the full details of chief executive compensation. Staff must provide this information on request — usually through the already established board governance process.

After the board has done this preparatory work, it should draft a formal document outlining the compensation process. This is useful for legal reasons: For example, in helping establish the "rebuttable presumption of reasonableness" protecting board members of 501(c)(3) and (c)(4) organizations from personal liability for compensation found to violate intermediate sanctions regulations, it will also provide some protection to boards of other types of nonprofits. From a practical standpoint, a formal document can also serve as a more detailed checklist for the board or compensation committee. The first part of the document should outline the relationship between chief executive compensation and the organization's mission. These details will be discussed further in subsequent chapters.

USING CONSULTANTS

Compensation consultants can help boards understand the market and assist them in negotiating the complexities of executive compensation plans. A compensation consultant is a neutral advisor who can offer knowledge and experience gleaned from many different organizations. By using a consultant who is experienced in, and knowledgeable about, nonprofit compensation practices, the board can receive additional assurance that it properly understands the marketplace and its options for setting compensation. The prospective chief executive can also be assured that he or she is being paid at a level that is appropriate to the marketplace.

Some nonprofit organizations might, therefore, be well served by a compensation consultant. However, final responsibility for establishing, monitoring, and ensuring the appropriateness of executive compensation rests with the board.

If you decide to use a compensation consultant, the first step is to determine the expertise the organization needs. The consultant should have experience in designing chief executive compensation for the nonprofit sector and ideally for the organization's particular part of the nonprofit sector. The consultant should have a good understanding of base salary, incentive, and deferred compensation options. He or she should fully understand, and have experience with, the intermediate sanctions regulations.

One of the best ways of assessing these qualifications is through references and referrals from other similar organizations. The references should cover the following:

- Timeliness and good project management

- Ability to work with staff, senior management, and the board

- Integrity, commitment, and technical competence

Once a consultant is hired, the lines of reporting and responsibility should be made clear. While the consultant may work closely with the organization's staff, the consultant's client must be the board, and the board should designate a single contact or small working group to manage the relationship. The board should then give the consultant a clear and complete project plan and access to relevant documents and information.

It is the consultant's duty to present the board with a comprehensible and competent analysis and recommendation. The board member(s) working with the consultant must provide adequate instructions and feedback to ensure that the product delivered by the consultant meets this standard. The consultant should also be available to meet with the full board to explain all findings and recommendations once they are made.

FUNDAMENTALS OF THE BOARD-CONSULTANT RELATIONSHIP:

1. Prospective consultants may be identified by the compensation committee or another subcommittee; it is advisable that the full board be informed of, and consulted on, the final hiring decision. The compensation committee or other designated members of the board should give the consultant direct guidance on what is needed.

2. The board should use the consultant as a resource as fully as possible, asking what the consultant thinks, what the consultant would recommend, and what the consultant believes are the advantages and disadvantages of taking a particular action under consideration.

3. The board should use the consultant to probe and challenge members' assumptions, and should also probe and challenge the consultant's assumptions.

4. Designated members of the board should review drafts of the consultant's reports before they are presented to the full board for consideration.

SUMMARY: ACTION STEPS FOR THE BOARD

- Ensure the board understands the role its mission, fiduciary, and legal responsibilities must play in setting chief executive compensation.

- Assign a body to oversee chief executive compensation.

  o Depending on circumstances, this body may be the compensation committee, the executive committee, or the full board.

  o We strongly recommend that, regardless of which body has primary oversight, final review and approval of chief executive compensation rest with the full board.

- Ensure that board members understand and are able to justify compensation decisions. Pay attention to the questions in the Form 990 concerning compensation and the board's role in reviewing it.

- The board chair should coordinate the process and ensure that members and committees are fulfilling their assigned responsibilities.

- Ensure that any board members with a conflict of interest are excluded from compensation decisions.

- Ensure that the board has complete and accurate information on the compensation received by the chief executive and other relevant senior staff.

- Draft a formal document outlining the compensation process.

- This helps boards establish a "rebuttable presumption of reasonableness," a protection from liability for organizations subject to IRS intermediate sanctions regulations.

- A formal document also serves as a guide for members to follow through the process.

- Review governance procedures and structure regularly, making changes as necessary. Consider using a consultant to assist the board in obtaining fair and accurate market information and expertise.

CHAPTER 2

ALIGNING COMPENSATION WITH ORGANIZATIONAL MISSION, GOALS, AND CULTURE

Once the board has designated the body (committee, task force, or whole board) that will be responsible for the compensation-setting process, the next step is to review the organization's mission, strategy, and performance goals. Understanding these will help the compensation committee determine the skills and qualities wanted in a chief executive, the appropriate level of chief executive compensation, the structure of the compensation plan, and the process for regular review of performance and compensation level. The compensation committee also needs to fully understand the organization's culture — the expectations, habits, and beliefs of the organization's key supporters and stakeholders.

Review of the organization's mission and strategy is a task for the full board. The board's goal should be to put on paper its current priorities for the organization and its key objectives for the next three to five years. This list should include major priorities and the objectives associated with them, along with a brief outline of the action steps that will be necessary to accomplish each objective. The list should be limited to four or five major priorities; targeting more than five priorities makes the goal-setting process unwieldy and can dilute the focus of the organization.

The strategic review need not be time-consuming, but a formal process, even a brief one, is helpful. A day or half-day spent thinking through strategic objectives and putting them on paper is highly recommended; a clear and focused set of priorities and objectives will help the compensation committee see what qualities, skills, and experience will be most important in the new chief executive. (Please see the Suggested Resources section at the back of this book for a list of titles helpful in the strategic planning process; see especially Berry, *Strategic Planning Workbook for Nonprofit Organizations*.)

MEASURING PERFORMANCE: THE BALANCED SCORECARD APPROACH

If a strategic plan is already in place, the board should review it to ensure that it will continue to be appropriate through the search process and under a new chief executive. If no plan is in place, or if a rethinking is in order, one effective option for the board is the balanced scorecard approach, which allows an organization to think about performance in terms of the critical areas of achievement for the organization. Robert Kaplan and David Norton of the Harvard Business School introduced the balanced scorecard in the early 1990s in recognition of the fact that financial performance measures alone do not necessarily ensure long-term organizational health.[14] The balanced scorecard organizes strategy and mission objectives into **four** primary areas of performance: customer (best understood as mission in the nonprofit context), financial, internal, and innovation and learning.

Many organizations and management advisors have found the balanced scorecard approach valuable. It works especially well in the nonprofit sector, where financial measures do not define organizational success because the organizational mission is not about making a profit. Using the balanced scorecard approach, a nonprofit organization might ask the following series of questions to define its objectives in the four performance areas:

Mission	Internal
Financial	Innovation and Learning

Mission: How effective are we in carrying out our mission? How satisfied are our stakeholders with our services? Have we had the expected impact on our mission?

How is the organization managing its relations with its stakeholders? How can the organization ensure that key stakeholders — members, donors, and others — remain committed to the organization's mission and provide tangible support?

Financial: Is the organization attaining its financial objectives? How effectively is the organization using its financial resources to accomplish its mission? How much and in what ways must the financial picture change in order for the organization to more effectively achieve its overall mission and its nonfinancial objectives? What additional financial resources are needed to further our mission? What return on investment relative to our mission goals are we getting from our resources?

Internal: How effectively does the organization operate? Do internal operations effectively enable the organization to carry out its mission? How does the organization need to improve its internal operations in order to better achieve its mission? How well is the organization being led? How capable is our workforce of meeting our mission?

Innovation and learning: What must the organization do to ensure that it can continue to be viable in the future? In what ways has the organization been growing, and in what ways has it been stagnant or shrinking? In what areas is growth desirable, and what must the organization do to initiate and sustain that growth?

[14] Robert S. Kaplan and David P. Norton, *Translating Strategy into Action: The Balanced Scorecard* (Boston: Harvard Business School Press, 1996).

A We recommend an annual chief executive performance review tied to the board governance process. The best way to link compensation to performance is to decide before the evaluation the rewards associated with achieving your organization's objectives. Thus, you could agree with the chief executive that achieving stated objectives would mean (finances allowing) a certain percentage increase in salary, or the award of an incentive amount, or some combination of the two. Going beyond the objectives would be worth more.

We also recommend that objectives be set in three categories: strategic objectives (the Harvard Balanced Scorecard approach is useful for deciding on strategic objectives), performance against unanticipated challenges, and leadership. Objectives may be given different weightings (i.e., be worth a different percentage of the overall assessment) based on their importance to the organization. Measures for achieving success should be as concrete as possible.

In the absence of an existing link between pay and performance, the next best thing is to decide on an appropriate reward (a salary increase, an ad hoc bonus, or some combination of the two) and carefully explain to the chief executive the particular achievements that justify the boost in pay. That explanation could then serve as the basis for the following year's performance plan.

Remember that any bonus or salary increase must not increase compensation by so much that it creates intermediate sanctions concerns.

UNDERSTANDING ORGANIZATIONAL CULTURE

Reflection on the organization's culture is another important aspect of the initial review of strategy and objectives. The organization's mission, its founders' vision, and the attitudes of its staff and supporters all may contribute to an understanding of its culture, and the constraints that the culture may put on the compensation level and plan for its chief executive. Organizations with a religious background, for example, may be uncomfortable with fully market-based levels of compensation — even when compared to other comparable religious organizations — but certainly with respect to general nonprofit compensation. Charities can sometimes be uncomfortable with including an incentive element in the compensation package. Many nonprofits (social advocacy organizations, for example) have an egalitarian ethos that may make them uncomfortable with a large difference between chief executive pay and that of other staff. Some may look for a multiple between the pay of the highest paid and lowest paid employee. If the organization applies a multiple, it may have to either restrain chief executive pay (and risk problems in recruitment and retention) or increase the pay of the lowest paid (perhaps to above-market levels).

Numerous nonprofits also pride themselves on being informal and un-bureaucratic; such organizations may resist a highly structured compensation and performance review process. A compensation committee that tries to impose a compensation level or plan inconsistent with the organizational culture could find itself alienating key staff members and outside stakeholders.

In order to understand the organization's culture, the compensation committee can interview key staff members and long-serving board members. The existing staff compensation system may also be an indicator of the organizational culture. If salaries are generally low compared to the market, this may reflect a service ethos that might be at odds with a more aggressive chief executive compensation package. Of course, low salaries may also reflect an organization's financial situation, or simple organizational inertia. The absence of a coherent compensation system may also reflect an organization's conscious choice of an informal operating style. With the new 990 reporting requirements asking for the disclosure of more employees' compensation, organizations with an informal compensation system may, however, find it harder to explain or defend their compensation decisions.

APPLYING THE BOARD'S UNDERSTANDING MISSION AND CULTURE

When the review of organizational priorities and culture is complete, the compensation committee should then consider the implications for the chief executive position. In doing so, the committee may want to use the following questions as a guide:

- What constraints does the organizational culture put on chief executive compensation in terms of level of compensation and acceptable compensation structure?

- Do the values and attitudes of the organizations from which a new chief executive might be recruited — and hence the values and attitudes an individual from those organizations would bring to the chief executive role — align with those of your organization?

- What are the values and attitudes of the organization's particular sector of the nonprofit world and its stakeholders?

- What qualities are desirable in the chief executive? Does the organization need someone who is primarily a leader and external voice of the organization? A manager? A fundraiser? A mission specialist?

- How much and what kind of experience is required in the chief executive?

- What is the financial situation of the organization? How is the level of compensation that can be offered affected by the organization's financial constraints?

- In defining the marketplace for the chief executive, it is important to consider both which organizations are most like it in terms of mission, scope, and geography, and where an organization might look to recruit a new chief executive.

- Will the organization recruit a new chief executive from other nonprofits (and if so, which types)?

- Will it recruit from the for-profit sector (and what part of it)? (It is not advisable — or possible, in most cases — to set compensation at a level competitive with the for-profit sector, for cultural, financial, and legal reasons).

- To what nonprofit organizations might your organization lose the current chief executive (these are organizations that help define the market for the chief executive)? Should your organization set compensation to be competitive with these organizations (again, it is not advisable to set compensation at for-profit levels, even if the for-profit sector is a potential hiring source or next career step for your chief executive)?

- Would the organization's mission and values be better served by recruiting from within the organization?

The following three examples illustrate different ways in which a board's review of organizational priorities and culture can affect compensation decisions.

Organization A is a social service agency that serves impoverished citizens in a major city. It has grown rapidly over the past 10 years and has become recognized as a leading contributor to the well-being of the city's poorer citizens. However, over the past year, whistleblowing by two staff members and an inquiry by the board have led to charges that the executive director and another staff member embezzled significant amounts from the organization. As a result of the ensuing negative publicity, Organization A has lost a significant portion of its donor base as well as much of its credibility with the public.

The board realizes that its first priority must be to downsize the organization so that it can continue to function with reduced levels of financial support and regain some measure of public trust. For the new executive director, the board's search committee thus seeks someone who can manage a staff and facility restructuring, develop a stronger public relations program than the current limited one, and find ways to reduce administrative costs — and one who is willing to accept a relatively low level of compensation while doing so, with the recognition that success could enable higher compensation at some future date.

Organization B is a new nonprofit organization dedicated to the publication and dissemination of the religious writings of Reverend Smith, who is leaving his current position as head pastor of a large church to found the organization and serve as its chief executive. At the church, Reverend Smith's compensation as head pastor had been set by a board of laypersons in the congregation. The board had set compensation based on the compensation received by the pastors of other churches in the same region with congregations of similar size. The board of Organization B will consist primarily of members from the church's board. Given that Organization B has a different mission, its board will have to determine a different marketplace for Reverend Smith, incorporating data for nonprofit publishing and media organizations. However, it must maintain consistency with a religious mission, and reflect the expectations of the board members and other congregants of the church (who in large part will constitute the audience for Organization B). These key stakeholders may be uncomfortable with a large increase in compensation.

Organization C is a nationwide membership association. It has a strong program that combines member benefits such as reduced-price insurance and travel opportunities with quality professional development opportunities for members, and as a result has built a steady and loyal membership. With the retirement of the longtime chief executive, C's board has a chance to evaluate the association's situation. As a result, the board identifies a major shortcoming in the association's operations: It is not serving its members as well as it could because it has no strategic plan for advocacy at the federal or state level. It is not playing the role it should in identifying and responding to political issues that affect its members.

C's board sets two priorities, with associated objectives:

1. A mission priority, to serve its members more effectively by adding advocacy to its activities; objectives include developing an advocacy policy within a year, and identifying existing connections in national and state political circles within six months.

2. A learning priority, to develop board and staff understanding of the workings of advocacy; objectives include hiring a consultant to provide guidance in the development of this new area.

C's compensation committee then connects these new priorities with its chief executive search process. Because existing programs are already efficiently managed by lower-level staff, and because development of the advocacy aspect will be a major leap for the organization, committee members agree that the new chief executive should be someone who can spearhead an expanded or new advocacy effort. This in turn has implications for the kinds of connections and background that the committee will seek in the new chief executive, and therefore for the compensation level that will be required to attract the right person.

These examples portray some of the ways that the larger organizational picture can affect a compensation committee's decisions. Once it has reviewed the organization's priorities, goals, and culture, and ascertained their implications for the chief executive's profile and compensation, the compensation committee can address the next steps in the process: developing a title, job description, and profile for the position; creating a compensation philosophy that formally articulates the principles that will guide the board in setting compensation; and determining the marketplace for the position.

SUMMARY: ACTION STEPS FOR THE BOARD

- Review the organization's mission and strategy to ensure that the chief executive possesses the appropriate skills and that compensation is aligned with organizational culture and the appropriate marketplace.

- Document strategic objectives.

  o Boards may wish to consult the Harvard Balanced Scorecard, which organizes objectives into four categories: mission, financial, internal, and innovation and learning.

  o Review and documentation of strategic objectives should be a formal process, with the participation of the full board. It need not be lengthy though; a full day of focused discussion should be sufficient.

- Consult appropriate resources to ensure that the board fully understands the organization's culture.

  o Interviews with key staff or long-serving board members and the current compensation system may provide insight.

- Consider how mission and culture affect the qualifications required in a chief executive and the level of compensation the organization's mission and culture will support.

CHAPTER 3

ESTABLISHING THE TITLE, JOB DESCRIPTION, AND PROFILE

Having defined the organization's priorities and objectives, and assessed the chief executive's role in meeting those objectives, the compensation committee next needs to formally define the chief executive position. It should do so by drafting a new job description or updating an existing one. The job description outlines the duties and most important responsibilities of the chief executive position. A good position description will aid the compensation committee in defining performance expectations and the qualities desired in a candidate for the position. It will also support the annual review of the chief executive (especially if that person has been in office for some time).

In some cases the compensation committee may also need to designate the chief executive's title. A nonprofit chief executive may be called executive director, director, administrator, president, or chief executive officer (CEO). There is no bright-line distinction among these titles, but the ways in which they are customarily used can provide a guideline.

- In community service organizations and membership organizations such as associations, the chief executive is most often called executive director. This title conveys the sense that the person is leading the staff in carrying out a service mission.

- In cultural and arts institutions, the chief executive is often called director, as in the director of a museum. However, where confusion with another use of the term may occur (as in a theater), many organizations use executive director instead.

- In education, the chief executive of a university or college is the president, and the chief executive of a private elementary or secondary school is the headmaster, headmistress, head of school, or principal. These titles differentiate the chief executive, whose work focuses on overall leadership and external relations, from the dean, whose work focuses more on internal matters.

- In health care, the chief executive of a hospital is often called administrator, a title that reflects the managerial and fiscal responsibilities of the position.

- In professional societies where the board sees itself as the actual leadership of the organization, the term executive director is often used for the internal leader of the organization

- In other types of nonprofits, especially larger ones, president and CEO are commonly used to designate the chief executive. These titles, especially when combined, convey a sense of the person's overall leadership role in the organization.

In fact, more and more nonprofits are designating their chief executives as president or chief executive. As Richard Chait, William Ryan, and Barbara Taylor point out, this reflects changes both in chief executive and in stakeholder expectations:

> Yesterday's naïve nonprofit administrator or executive director has become today's sophisticated president or CEO, titles that betray changes in the stature, perception, and professionalism of the positions…. Many executives have earned graduate degrees in nonprofit management…. More important, nonprofit executives have acquired what formal education alone cannot confer: standing as organizational leaders (a status often underscored by the compensation package). As a result, trustees, employees, clients, and donors expect far more of nonprofit CEOs today than a genial personality, moral probity, managerial acumen, and a passionate commitment to the organization's social mission. Stakeholders, in a word, expect leadership.[15]

In the final analysis, however, the choice of title will depend on the preferences of the board, the history and culture of the organization, and the preferences of the person holding or seeking the position.

The title and job description should reflect the strategic objectives that the organization hopes to achieve in hiring the chief executive. One organization might emphasize fundraising over internal management; for another, external representation might be especially important. The drafting of the job description therefore provides the first opportunity to establish performance expectations that are in line with the organization's priorities and objectives.

MAJOR ELEMENTS OF A CHIEF EXECUTIVE JOB DESCRIPTION

It is a mistake simply to take an off-the-shelf chief executive job description and use it without review. (Nevertheless, we have provided an example in Appendix IV.) While the elements of a chief executive job description are likely to be similar across organizations, the emphasis placed on those elements will not be. Nor should an organization simply reuse an existing job description. Before hiring a new chief executive, the organization should carefully review any existing job description to make sure it still accurately reflects the organization's priorities and goals. Are the responsibilities clearly defined and measurable? Have changes in the organization's mission or changes in the environment created new challenges and responsibilities for the executive? What are the most important challenges the organization will face going forward? What will be the most important responsibilities and leadership

---

[15] Richard P. Chait, William P. Ryan, and Barbara E. Taylor, *Governance as Leadership* (Hoboken, NJ: John Wiley & Sons, 2005), pp. 2–3.

requirements of the chief executive in leading the organization to achieve success? The board should never forget that a good job description for the chief executive will clearly define the chief executive's role with respect to the role of the board.

As it begins to develop its chief executive job description, the compensation committee should look to the chief executive's major responsibilities and to the qualifications required by the position.

QUESTIONNAIRE 1: WHAT ARE THE MAJOR RESPONSIBILITIES OF THE CHIEF EXECUTIVE IN MEETING ORGANIZATIONAL CHALLENGES?

1. What are the most significant external challenges that the organization will face in the next three to five years? Internal challenges?

2. What will the chief executive need to do to meet those challenges successfully?

3. Prioritize the activities below in terms of their relative importance, given the challenges facing the organization. For each area, describe the results that you expect the chief executive to achieve.

_____ Achieving the organization's mission: vision and planning for the future of the organization

_____ Leadership of the organization; providing a clear direction for staff

_____ Relations with supporters, stakeholders, donors

_____ Advocacy/representing the organization to the public

_____ Internal management of the organization, including personnel management

_____ Fundraising and development

_____ Financial health of the organization

_____ Working with the board, including

  • Informing the board of the organization's state of affairs

  • Advising it on important issues

  • Executing its directions

  • Board development

_____ Other:

4. Given your answer to #3, what will be the two or three most important responsibilities of the chief executive?

Using the answers to each element of the questionnaire, the compensation committee can develop a list of duties to be included in the chief executive job description. The list of duties in the job description may be built on the elements in the following list, sequenced in accordance with their relative priority for the specific organization:

- **Mission role:** State the organization's mission and goals, and outline the specific steps that the chief executive will take to achieve them.

- **Leadership role:** State the role that the chief executive will play in relationship to the board, including advising the board and assisting with board development; conducting strategic planning and implementing strategic plans; and acting as the organization's chief visionary, positioning the organization for future effectiveness.

- **Public role:** Outline the ways in which the chief executive will represent the organization and lead outreach to the public and to the organization's stakeholders.

- **Administrative role:** Describe the chief executive's role in overseeing the design, promotion, and delivery of the programs, products, and services of the organization.

- **Human resources role:** Describe the ways in which the chief executive will build and maintain human capital, including recruiting and retaining quality staff, leading the organization in improving the skills of staff members, and recruiting and retaining an effective corps of volunteers.

- **Fiscal role:** Outline the chief executive's role in ensuring the financial integrity and health of the organization, including managing organizational resources, leading the annual and multiyear budget process, overseeing financial management and effective cost control, and ensuring compliance with government and internal financial controls and requirements.

- **Development role:** Outline the chief executive's role in fundraising, including setting goals, organizing the fundraising effort, and, where appropriate, acting as the organization's chief fundraiser.

- **Role in working with the board:** Explain how the chief executive will advise, inform, and support the board in leading the organization.

Using the list of chief executive duties, the board should then complete the job description with a summary of the skills and experience required for the position.

One great danger in this process is that the compensation committee will come out of it with a profile that only a divine being could match. To avoid the "in spare time, walks on water" syndrome, committee members should limit their consideration to the two or three most important elements in the job description and the two or three greatest challenges that lie ahead, and should identify only two or three attributes in response to each of the other questions. Doing so will help committee members separate essential characteristics from those they can get along without.

The following questionnaire may be helpful in guiding the committee as it identifies the most important characteristics of the chief executive.

QUESTIONNAIRE 2: WHAT CHARACTERISTICS ARE MOST IMPORTANT FOR CONSIDERATION IN FINDING THE RIGHT CHIEF EXECUTIVE?

1. Consider the two or three most important elements in the chief executive job description, and the most important challenges facing the organization. What are the most critical characteristics (skills, capabilities, experience, and background) that the chief executive will need to have to perform his or her duties?

2. What are the critical personal values that the chief executive of this organization must have to be successful?

3. What past experience, education, and training must the chief executive have?

4. Which attributes of the current chief executive contribute most to his or her success in the position? Why?

5. Will these same attributes be equally critical for the next chief executive? What might change?

SUMMARY: ACTION STEPS FOR THE BOARD

- Identify the most important duties and responsibilities of the chief executive position, informed by the organization's mission and strategic objectives.

- Identify the most important skills, capabilities, experience, background, and education required for the position.

- Create or update, as necessary, the position description for the chief executive.

- The position description should reflect realistic expectations of the qualities possessed by current or potential chief executives by including only those qualities that are key to the organization.

- Ensure that the chief executive's title is appropriate for the organization.

CHAPTER 4

DEVELOPING A COMPENSATION PHILOSOPHY

An organization's compensation philosophy lays out the values, principles, and guidelines for the organization's overall compensation structure and supporting systems. The compensation philosophy should apply to the entire organization, not just the chief executive.

A formal compensation philosophy provides several benefits to an organization. It ensures that the board explicitly considers the most critical issues involved in defining appropriate compensation, including internal and external equity, impact on the organization's finances, and legal compliance issues. It allows compensation issues to be dealt with systematically and efficiently on an ongoing basis, both for the chief executive and throughout the organization. It allows compensation (e.g., salary and bonus budgets) to be factored into long-range financial planning. It provides the organization with legal protection insofar as it defines the organization's marketplace and documents the procedures for setting chief executive compensation in line with market practice (following market practice will help protect from intermediate sanctions liability). When an organization reaches consensus on its compensation philosophy before developing a new compensation structure or introducing new compensation-related systems, it is far less likely to encounter problems with perceived inequities and disparities later on. A well-thought-out compensation philosophy will also support the immediate goal of developing a chief executive compensation plan.

A good compensation philosophy is based on an understanding of the organization's strategic goals and culture. In terms of process, a draft compensation philosophy is probably best developed by a small task force that is part of the compensation committee or the full board; if a consultant has been retained to advise on the chief executive search, he or she can help in drafting the philosophy. The draft should then be presented to the full board for approval. The board has ultimate responsibility for the compensation philosophy.

The task force should work together with the current chief executive in developing the compensation philosophy, which should apply to the entire organization. The chief executive is more directly involved than the board in the activities of the organization. Therefore, he or she has a firsthand understanding of the organization's culture and values, is more likely to be aware of any dissatisfaction among staff with current compensation arrangements, and may have a better understanding of the organization's marketplace. In the absence of a current chief executive, the task force should consult senior staff members who understand the organization's history, culture, and expectations.

The compensation philosophy should cover the following:

1. The objectives of the compensation plan. Examples of objectives are

   - To reflect and promote the organization's mission and values

   - To support the organization's strategies for carrying out its mission

   - To enable the organization to attract, motivate, and retain the executive talent needed to carry out its mission

   - To achieve the above goals within the financial constraints of the organization

2. The appropriate marketplace for the organization. For example, a marketplace can generally include a blend of the following:

   - Organizations that have similar missions, stakeholders, and funding sources.

   - The same geographic focus and recruitment sources: national, regional, local or international

   - Organizations with similar scope (e.g., budget and staff size). For example:

     o Arts organizations with budgets between $10 million and $50 million located in major metropolitan areas

     o Undergraduate colleges in California and the Pacific Coast region with enrollments under 2,000 students, recruiting regionally

3. The organization's desired position in the marketplace: how competitively the organization wishes to pay

   - This may simply be a statement that the entire compensation plan, including its cash compensation and benefits will be competitive with the marketplace in order to attract, motivate, and retain the talent the organization needs to successfully carry out its mission.

   - A compensation philosophy may also specify how competitively compensation will be set relative to the defined marketplace. For example:

     o The organization will pay base salaries at the median (or first quartile, or third quartile) of the marketplace. (See discussion of quartiles in the box on page 38.)

     o The organization will pay total cash (base pay plus any bonus or incentive) for exceptional performance at no greater than the 50th (or 25th, or 75th) percentile of the marketplace.

4. Whether and how compensation will be linked to performance and other factors. For example:

   - Compensation will reward outstanding performers and provide appropriate signals to staff members needing improvement.

- Compensation will be linked to an annual performance management process, with individual and organizational goals.

- Compensation adjustments will be based on achievement of those goals.

5. Whether and how variable compensation, such as incentive compensation, bonus compensation, or other pay-at-risk elements will be incorporated into the compensation system. For example:

- The compensation structure will (will not) include incentive and other reward systems where appropriate to the organization's marketplace.

- The chief executive will have an annual incentive compensation opportunity of up to X percent (or "consistent with market practice") based on established organizational goals and a board rating of his or her leadership during the past year.

6. The degree of formality and structure with which the organization is comfortable. For example:

- The compensation structure will be based on a single set of salary ranges; or salaries appropriate to professional areas/positions will be individually matched to the marketplace.

7. The governance structure and process for setting and adjusting compensation, including the steps necessary for meeting IRS legal standards. For example:

- The compensation committee will set compensation for the chief executive.

- The compensation committee will review, on an annual basis, compensation of the chief executive and other employees considered to be "disqualified persons" under IRS "intermediate sanctions" to ensure compliance with intermediate sanctions and any other rules and regulations.

- The compensation committee will review, on an annual basis, the budgets for salary increases and bonus/incentive pay (if any).

- The compensation committee will review, every ___ year(s), compensation levels and structure for the organization as a whole, to ensure their compliance with the compensation philosophy.

- The compensation committee will ensure that compensation is reasonable with respect to IRS and stakeholder scrutiny.

8. Other characteristics of the compensation system. For example:

- The system will be clearly and regularly communicated to staff.

- The structure will take into account community standards and the organization's role in the community (such as its faith-based origins).

- Compensation for the chief executive will be consistent with the compensation philosophy set for the rest of the organization.

EXPLANATION OF PERCENTILES/QUARTILES

In determining how competitive pay will be, an organization's compensation philosophy will usually target pay at a certain *percentile* or *quartile* of the market. This is done because (1) percentiles and quartiles measure the proportion of data in a group that falls above and below a certain number, and thus allow an organization to position itself relative to others in its marketplace, and (2) the surveys that serve as a major source for setting compensation for chief executives and other positions (see Chapter 5) typically report market data in terms of percentiles or — especially — quartiles.

Percentiles indicate what percentage of data fall below a certain data point. For example, if the 10th percentile is $50,000, then 10 percent of the data fall below $50,000 (and thus, 90 percent is above $50,000).

Quartiles divide the data into four groups of equal size. When used in the context of a salary survey, "quartile" refers to the upper limit of the group in question. The first quartile, then, is equivalent to the 25th percentile; 25 percent (or one-fourth) are below this point, and 75 percent (three-fourths) are above. The second quartile, or 50th percentile, is usually referred to as the **median**. All of these three terms mean the same thing: that half of the data is below, and half is above, the data point in question. The third quartile, or 75th percentile, is higher than 75 percent of the data, and lower than 25 percent. If a "fourth quartile" is reported, it represents the highest data point, or maximum.

Note that the median is not the same as the mean or average of the data. The mean is calculated by adding all the data together, and dividing by the number of data points. The mean can thus be skewed by outliers. Therefore, the median is generally a better representation of the midpoint of the market.

In the sample compensation philosophy that follows, "compensation system" refers to the overall system for managing pay and benefits, assessing performance, and integrating compensation with organizational strategy and objectives. "Compensation structure" refers to the formal mechanisms that are part of the compensation system, including the hierarchy of salaries and other benefits that apply to employees of the organization. The purpose of the philosophy is to articulate the principles that govern the structure and the elements that will be included in the system, not to specify their exact nature; for this reason, the philosophy does not describe the hierarchy of positions within the organization, the amounts of base pay and incentives, or the specific parameters for conducting performance evaluation.

With its chief executive profile and compensation philosophy in place, the compensation committee will be in a position to investigate the marketplace from which it will draw its pool of chief executive candidates.

SAMPLE COMPENSATION PHILOSOPHY
(APPLIES TO THE ENTIRE ORGANIZATION, INCLUDING THE CHIEF EXECUTIVE)

- The compensation structure and systems of our organization will support our mission, strategy, and values.

- Organization XYZ will pay for performance; skills and competencies; development and growth; and effective visible commitment to the organization.

- The compensation system will encourage recruitment, retention, and motivation of outstanding employees so that the organization can achieve its mission and objectives.

- The compensation system will reward truly outstanding performers and provide appropriate feedback to staff members who need improvement.

- The compensation structure will be a mixture of base salary; performance-based "at risk" pay appropriate to the nonprofit marketplace; retirement and other benefits; and special recognition awards where merited by performance.

- A portion of each employee's pay will be tied to the achievement of organizational and individual objectives. Unusual individual achievement may also merit special financial awards.

- The compensation system will include annual adjustments to pay ranges based on changes in the marketplace (subject to financial constraints). Adjustments to individual base pay will be based on job performance and growth in mastering job competencies. All adjustments to pay will be consistent with practice in the nonprofit marketplace.

- Compensation for the chief executive will be set by the compensation committee of the board with review by the full board, which will comply with all applicable legal standards. The compensation committee will regularly review the compensation of the chief executive and all other employees considered to be "disqualified persons" under IRS "intermediate sanctions" regulations, to ensure compliance with the regulations and any other rules and regulations to which the board is subject regarding compensation.

- The compensation system will have a coherent structure based on pay practices consistent with our nonprofit mission and status, but will recognize that parts of our organization are in different markets and that the compensation for each position must be based on the appropriate marketplace for that professional area.

- Organization XYZ will pay as close as possible to the median (midpoint) of the appropriate external marketplace, while recognizing that internal equity and financial constraints can justify some deviation from the market.

- The marketplace adequacy of the structure will be judged in terms of total compensation, including benefits; the total package will be competitive with the marketplace.

- The compensation structure will be linked to an effective performance management system with individual growth and development as well as professional achievement goals. The goals will be accompanied by effective benchmarks for measuring success.

  - The board will review chief executive performance on an annual basis. Performance objectives for the coming year will be determined jointly by the chief executive and the board at the annual board meeting, with the explicit understanding that salary adjustments and any incentive opportunity will be based on performance against these objectives. Salary will be adjusted based on inflation/market movement and performance. Any incentive earned will be awarded based on performance.

  - The chief executive will annually prepare and submit to the board a self-assessment of performance as input to the performance review.

  - The board will clearly outline and communicate how performance will be linked to salary adjustments and any incentive opportunity. There will be clear measures for achieving success in each objective, and these will be linked to levels of award. Salary adjustments and any incentive opportunity will be based on market practice. The board will ensure that no salary adjustment or incentive award will cause total compensation to exceed amounts that are reasonable for IRS standards.

- The board retains the right to withhold adjustments at its discretion, regardless of performance.

- Compensation will be fair and transparent.

- Compensation will be reasonable and defensible relative to IRS regulations and stakeholder expectations.

- Executives and staff will receive regular and comprehensive training in the compensation system.

Summary: Action Steps for the Board

- Ensure that the board understands the purpose and benefits of a compensation philosophy, and that the compensation philosophy reflects the organization's mission, culture, and objectives.

- Create or review the organization's compensation philosophy.

  o We recommend that the creation of a draft compensation philosophy be assigned to a small task force within the compensation committee or board.

  o If possible, the entity charged with drafting the compensation philosophy should solicit the input of the chief executive; in the absence of the chief executive, knowledgeable senior staff should be consulted.

  o Remember that the compensation philosophy should apply to the entire organization.

- Ensure that the compensation philosophy covers the items listed on page 36.

- Once the final compensation philosophy has been drafted, it should be reviewed and approved by the full board.

CHAPTER 5
UNDERSTANDING THE MARKETPLACE

The compensation committee's next task is to understand the marketplace. The committee should understand the nonprofit marketplace in general, as well as the specific marketplace for the organization. In some cases it may also be appropriate to understand aspects of the for-profit marketplace, especially for those nonprofits (health care organizations, for example) that may compete for talent with the for-profit sector.

For reasons of both law and custom, the nonprofit marketplace is more constrained in its pay practices than the for-profit market with which some board members may be more familiar. Even where there is some degree of for-profit competition for executive talent, a nonprofit board should focus first on nonprofit practices. The specific nonprofit marketplace for the organization can set further limits — again both in terms of customary practice and legal requirements — on both the level of compensation and on the kind of compensation structure that is appropriate.

Some organizations will choose to retain a compensation consultant to help analyze the organization's marketplace. A consultant's experience, understanding of the local market, and access to relevant data sources can help a compensation committee understand its options. A set of guidelines for hiring a compensation consultant can be found in Chapter 1.

Whether or not a consultant is retained, the board is ultimately responsible for the compensation decision, and therefore should have a basic understanding of the relevant marketplace. IRS regulations require the board to make a reasoned judgment on executive compensation. Executive compensation must meet the legal standard of "the value that would ordinarily be paid for like services by like enterprises under like circumstances."[16] If a board considers data that are sufficiently detailed and reflective of the organization's particular marketplace to allow such a reasoned judgment to be made, it can qualify (if it is a 501(c)(3) or (c)(4) organization) for a "rebuttable presumption of reasonableness" that can help it avoid potential IRS penalties under the intermediate sanctions regulations (see Chapter 6 for further discussion of the rebuttable presumption of reasonableness for intermediate sanctions purposes). A board that already has some understanding of the relevant market will be in a better position to judge the suitability of the data with which it is presented.

---

[16] Internal Revenue Service, *Instructions for Form 990 2008*, pp. 65–66.

A Yes, incentive-based compensation for the chief executive of a nonprofit is legal, and it is an increasingly common practice among nonprofits. Many nonprofits find incentives an effective way to link chief executive pay to organizational performance and objectives. The total amount of compensation, including the incentive, must be consistent with market practice, however, to meet the intermediate sanctions and related legal standards.

THE NONPROFIT MARKETPLACE

As noted in the introduction, nonprofit salaries rose significantly at many organizations during the late 1990s and through 2008. Pay practices such as bonus and deferred compensation, formerly seen only in for-profit organizations, became increasingly common in nonprofit organizations, although varying by kind of nonprofit (very common among associations and larger charities and cultural institutions, less common among academic institutions, advocacy organizations, and foundations).[17] Nevertheless, pay in the nonprofit sector remains below that of the for-profit sector, especially at the top of the organization. Even chief executives who expect competitive pay do not — and should not — generally expect that their nonprofit compensation will equal what they could earn in the for-profit world. Earning money is not the mission of nonprofits. Most nonprofit employees — and all good nonprofit chief executives — get their deepest job satisfaction from helping their organizations achieve their missions.

Historically, the nonprofit sector has been particularly conservative in its approach to non-base pay (e.g., bonus or incentive) compensation. But times have changed. Boards now use bonus or incentive compensation to motivate executives to achieve performance goals. They have also recognized that putting some compensation "at risk" (i.e., dependent on meeting performance expectations, and hence not guaranteed) helps the staff manage costs. Before making extra cash compensation part of a chief executive compensation package, however, boards need to be sure that such an arrangement will be acceptable within their particular marketplace, as well as consistent with their organization's culture and expectations. Furthermore, they need to recognize that there is only so much total compensation the marketplace will justify. All elements of a compensation plan, including the value of incentive, deferred compensation, and benefits must add to a total compensation amount that is within market practice. Thus adding incentive compensation dollars or deferred compensation awards can mean controlling or even reducing base salary.

Total compensation must be controlled in part for legal reasons, but also in order to protect the organization's reputation with stakeholders, staff, and the public. The public expects that the compensation levels at a nonprofit will conform to practice in

---

[17] Surveys differ on the percentage of nonprofits that provide extra cash compensation to chief executives — see page 6. Since all surveys cited cover large and/or national nonprofits, the actual practice among all nonprofits is likely to be lower than the survey data suggest.

the nonprofit, not the for-profit, marketplace. Expectations for particular organizations may be even stronger — faith-based institutions, volunteer organizations, advocacy organizations, and others may have compensation expectations shaped by their history, membership, or donor base.

From a legal perspective, IRS regulations provide a general limit on the total amount of compensation, and they also limit deferral options, both as to types of deferral vehicles and to the amount that can be deferred in particular vehicles. Because there is no equity available in a nonprofit organization, boards should be wary of any compensation arrangement that looks like the distribution of revenues. Revenue-based compensation is discussed in detail in Chapter 8.

Q **What are the similarities and differences between compensation issues faced by nonprofit and for-profit organizations?**

A Both for-profits and nonprofits face the challenge of balancing the market for executive talent against their internal resources. Nonprofits increasingly are able to use many of the same tools as for-profits in paying their executives. They can use bonus and incentive pay if they wish, and are able to offer some forms of deferred compensation. As noted above, base salaries have risen in recent years.

Nevertheless, nonprofits continue to operate under stricter constraints than for-profit organizations. As a result, total compensation at nonprofits remains generally below for-profit levels. Nonprofits face stronger public scrutiny and special legal oversight, through the IRS intermediate sanctions rules and other legal limits on compensation. Nonprofits cannot offer some of the most lucrative features of for-profit compensation, such as equity. Deferred compensation is subject to different, and stricter, rules for nonprofits. Bonus plans are less common, and when they exist, generally not as rich. Many nonprofits are also restrained in their pay practices by their mission, their culture, and donor and community expectations.

THE ORGANIZATION'S SPECIFIC MARKETPLACE

While nonprofit status by itself places some constraints on chief executive compensation, it is the particular marketplace for an organization that principally determines the upper and lower limits on what it can pay its chief executive. The IRS reasonableness standard provides a good definition of an organization's specific marketplace: "What would ordinarily be paid for like services by like enterprises under like circumstances."[18] When defining an organization's marketplace, compensation committee members should take the items in the box on page 46 into account.

---

[18] Internal Revenue Service, *Instructions for Form 990 2008,* p. 65.

No single factor alone determines the marketplace. The goal should be to specify the marketplace in terms of all the relevant factors. Thus, to take one example, the market for the chief executive of a museum in New York City might be defined by the following factors:

- Mission: Preservation and display of, and public education concerning, artifacts

- Recruitment sources: Museums, art galleries, university art departments

- Organization size: Budget between $15 and $25 million; approximately 200 employees

- Organization scope: National (that is, recruits nationally for the chief executive)

- Organization location: New York City

- Specific requirements: Must hold a Ph.D. in art history

- Service/experience: Must have served in senior positions for at least 10 years

This organization would then look for market data on organizations as close as possible to this description.

FACTORS TO CONSIDER WHEN DEFINING YOUR ORGANIZATION'S MARKETPLACE

- The organization's mission: Committee members should first consider which organizations are doing the same or similar types of work.

- Organization scope: Organizations should compare themselves to others of similar scope. Each sector has measures that are appropriate for defining its scope. For many organizations, budget and number of staff are good measures. Asset or endowment size is sometimes used also, such as for foundations or academic institutions. Membership might be used in organizations such as professional societies or associations. Standard surveys usually organize their data into budget and staff size groupings, for example, below $2.5 million, $2.5 to $5 million, $5 million to $10 million, and so on.

- Geographical reach: Does the organization work entirely at the local level? Is it statewide? Regional? National? International?

- Location: Where is the organization based? An organization may be located in a place with an unusually high or low cost of living that should be reflected in the salary. For example, compensation in certain metropolitan areas — such as San Francisco, New York City, Los Angeles, and Washington, D.C. — is generally above — in some cases significantly above — national market levels because of the extremely high cost of living in those places.

- Recruitment scope: An organization that works within a single locality may nevertheless recruit on a statewide, regional, or national basis (a museum, for example, may be based in a single city but be part of a nationwide marketplace for its director).

- The specific requirements for the position: The strategic analysis and job description should determine the specific and special needs for the position. Special technical skills can be a factor in determining the appropriate marketplace — for example, the chief executive must have an M.D. or be a lawyer, or have experience in media or information technology.

- Length of service and experience: In determining the appropriate marketplace for a serving chief executive, it is appropriate to look at organizations whose chief executives have comparable length of service and experience.

- Chief executive recruitment sources: Types of organizations from which a chief executive might be recruited, or to which he or she might go, can be included even if the missions of such organizations are somewhat different. The goal is to establish the market for the chief executive's services. A word of caution here: Although understanding recruitment sources can help in setting compensation, it does not determine compensation, especially when the candidates are being recruited from the for-profit sector. The fact that an executive from the for-profit sector is considered a viable candidate for a nonprofit position does not necessarily define the marketplace. Pay must always meet nonprofit market standards.

SOURCES OF MARKET INFORMATION

This section contains terms used by compensation professionals that may be unfamiliar to some. Please refer to the glossary for any needed assistance.

Market information comes from three sources: publicly available IRS data, publicly available surveys, and specially commissioned surveys.

IRS FORM 990 DATA

Form 990 filings are an obvious and easily obtainable source of compensation data on particular comparable organizations. A compensation committee can develop a list of organizations it sees as comparable and obtain information on their chief executive compensation with little effort or expense. But Form 990 data must be used carefully, especially data from the pre-2008 version of the form (see box on the next page). Nevertheless, 990 data, properly understood and adjusted for inflation, are valuable and accessible sources of information on the pay practices of comparable organizations.

Q How does budget size relate to the chief executive's salary?

A Budget size and chief executive pay correlate to some degree, and budget size is one of the factors that should be looked at as part of any market analysis. Budget size is also a factor that should be reviewed as part of any intermediate sanctions analysis.

That said, budget size by no means perfectly correlates with chief executive pay. Staff size, location, mission, the needs of the organization, its history and culture, and the qualifications and record of chief executive candidates can all affect chief executive pay in ways that swamp the budget size connection.

WORKING WITH FORM 990s

Data reported: Prior to the 2008 tax year, the form 990s asked, in Part V-A (Part VIII of the 990-PF, used by private foundations), for "compensation" and "contributions to employee benefit plans and deferred compensation" data for officers, directors, trustees, and key employees. "Compensation" referred to total cash compensation (base pay plus any bonus or incentive compensation). The "benefits" sum included all benefits, including deferred compensation. Thus, while the data were useful for understanding the marketplace for total cash compensation, they were not as helpful for understanding market practice on base pay or pay structure. The post-2008 990s require that the elements of compensation be reported separately, so long as compensation is above $150,000.

Deferred compensation: Deferred compensation data prior to 2008 were not always reliable. Organizations were required to report deferred compensation as it was accrued and when it was finally paid. This could lead to double counting, and the reporting of anomalously high compensation in the pay-out year. Deferred compensation that had accrued over several years was reported first at the time of accrual and then again when paid as a single very large lump sum. This was typically seen in the year in which a deferred compensation plan vests — either at the end of a contract term or when a chief executive retires. The post-2008 Form 990 explicitly allows the backing-out of previously reported deferred compensation. In the pre-2008 990, organizations may or may not have included a footnote explaining large deferred compensation amounts. One should be skeptical, however, when looking at a pre-2008 990, of a large spike in compensation for a single year. To avoid this, the authors will sometimes take the average of three years' data (aged, of course) for organizations that show large variation from year to year.

Accuracy in reporting: There is no guarantee that data from a pre-2008 990 has been reported accurately or consistently. The "contributions to employee benefit plans and deferred compensation" sum, in particular, is often lower relative to cash compensation than one would expect based on typical market practice, and, especially in the past, was occasionally left blank. Housing and the value of defined benefit pension plans have been often omitted. "Compensation" is generally more reliable. Because reporting inconsistencies and omissions will only very rarely increase reported compensation, and will typically have a dampening effect, a market comparison based on data from the pre-2008 Form 990 is an inherently conservative approach (i.e., it will tend to underestimate market compensation). The post-2008 Form 990 will require organizations to report different components of compensation separately (including base salary, bonus, deferred compensation, and benefits for employees earning $150,000 or more), and thus will contain more useful and more reliable data for market comparisons.

"Aging" the data: Form 990 data will almost always be at least a year old, and often two or more years old. Like all market data, it must therefore be adjusted for inflation/market movement (this is frequently referred to as "aging" the data; see discussion on page 56).

The IRS has substantially changed the Form 990, effective for the 2008 tax year (see Appendix I).[19] The changes are designed to ensure that nonprofit organizations report all compensation received by their highest paid staff members. The form also asks new questions on governance and compensation practice. Organizations must now describe in detail the processes used to establish and review compensation for executives. Organizations are required to answer specific questions about the use of independent compensation consultants, comparability data, and written policies.

The fact that the IRS now requires nonprofit organizations to report their compensation governance practices, including whether they meet the requirements for the "rebuttable presumption of reasonableness" under the intermediate sanctions regulations, is a strong signal that it favors such practices even though they are not, strictly speaking, legally required.

SURVEYS: PUBLICLY AVAILABLE AND PROPRIETARY

Compensation survey information is made available to the public by both for-profit and nonprofit organizations. A representative list of organizations publishing national survey data is included in the resource list at the end of this book. WorldatWork (www.worldatwork.org), formerly the American Compensation Association, is an excellent source of information on survey sources.

National surveys include

- General compensation surveys. Some general surveys will cover a range of professional areas; other will be restricted to a particular professional area (e.g., finance, law). General surveys will typically have a nonprofit cut of the data.

- Surveys of the general nonprofit market, covering a broad array of nonprofit jobs and types of nonprofits

- Surveys of specific types of organizations in the nonprofit sector (for example, foundations, museums, international aid organizations)

Local surveys will cover a single metropolitan area, a state, or a region; they may cover all organizations, all nonprofits, or a subset of nonprofits. In the Washington, D.C., area, for example, the National Capital Area Human Resources Association (HRA) publishes a detailed survey of Washington-area compensation that includes data cuts for nonprofit organizations and associations. Other cities may have similar surveys, although in the authors' experience none is as good as the HRA survey for the Washington area.

National surveys may also report data for a specific city or metropolitan area (data reported for an entire region is less useful, as compensation practices may differ widely within the region). Watson Wyatt, for example, publishes a survey of national compensation practices that reports data for nonprofits in specific cities and metropolitan areas. The American Society of Association Executives (ASAE)

---

[19] Internal Revenue Service, *Instructions for Form 990 2008*, pp.1–2.

publishes an annual survey of association pay that includes cuts for specific cities. Specialized salary surveys should be used carefully and thoughtfully to avoid inappropriate comparisons. The ASAE survey, in particular, seems to be used by a wide range of organizations; we have found instances where the data have been used by social service organizations or other charities. We generally advise against this, since association salaries are often higher than those of other nonprofits. However, if a particular position (other than a chief executive position) is likely to be filled from an association, ASAE may be a useful source of data for that position, regardless of the type of organization.

While not a published survey, GuideStar (www.guidestar.org) is an excellent resource for those interested in compensation at nonprofit organizations. GuideStar maintains a searchable online database of 4.6 million IRS Form 990s from nonprofit organizations, including financial information and downloadable 990 Forms, and offers a number of other products and services to aid with market research. There is a range of fees for GuideStar services.

Survey data must usually be purchased from the organization publishing the survey — costs can range from a modest fee for a local survey to much higher fees for the larger national surveys produced by the major compensation consulting firms. Special cuts of survey data are often available from the sponsoring organization, again for a fee. A special cut allows an organization to obtain data from the relevant subset of a larger group. Preferably, data from a minimum of eight to 10 organizations — and ideally a larger group — should be included to make the results more meaningful (note, however, that organizations with budgets below $1 million are legally allowed to use only three comparators).

Survey data are increasingly available in the form of an Internet database that allows the user to create special cuts of the data using multiple factors such as location, organization type, and organization size. ASAE and HRA both post online versions of their surveys that allow a subscriber to create special cuts.

Not all survey data are publicly available. Surveys are regularly conducted by groups of nonprofit organizations with a common marketplace for their internal use, and the data are, in principle, available only to participants. However, nonparticipants can sometimes obtain the data by promising to participate in the next survey, or by requesting it from a friendly organization taking part in the survey.

Discovering what survey data are available can be challenging. One problem is that nonprofits, which often have limited resources, may not be able to fund, or even participate in, surveys.

Here are some suggestions for obtaining assistance:

- Contact groups and associations that might have conducted, or know of, compensation studies. These include local or regional associations of nonprofits, as well as associations of particular types of nonprofits, such as foundation grantmakers.

- Do a Web search to find organizations that might collect compensation information for organizations of similar type or locality. Follow up with a phone call to help ensure that the organization is legitimate and that the data are up to date and reliable, and ask for references among other nonprofits.

- Ask similar organizations what survey data they know about or have. A group of similar organizations may be open to contracting for a targeted survey.

- Ask a compensation consultant for assistance. A good consultant will have access to the most important national surveys and will know how to find more specific surveys, such as by region or nonprofit type.

- Be cautious about using data from search firms and recruiters. While they may have a good feel for the current market, they do not typically conduct formal, research-based surveys. Their data may not represent the overall market, and may be skewed toward the organizations they are most familiar with or that are actively in the market and are able afford to hire a search firm.

- Avoid data available for free on the Web, unless the data come from a source that is known to be reputable. Free data are often self-reported without any check on accuracy and not always representative of the overall market.

CASH COMPENSATION

- Base pay or base salary compensation: The annual salary paid, excluding any extra cash compensation

- Extra cash compensation: Any bonus or incentive paid

- Total cash compensation: Salary plus any extra cash compensation

- Location: Compensation reported for organizations in a particular geographic area, generally a city, state, or region

- Organization type: General compensation surveys will have a nonprofit category, which may or may not be broken down further. Nonprofit surveys may be broken down by type of nonprofit. These types can include individual member or professional associations, trade associations, academic organizations, advocacy organizations, cultural institutions, and others.

- Organization budget: This is generally grouped by category, for example, less than $5 million, $5 million to $10 million, and so on. Some surveys will report revenues instead of budget. Since at nonprofit organizations revenues and budget must be roughly equivalent, revenues and budget can be used interchangeably.

- Time in position: The number of years incumbents have been in the position

- Number of employees: Usually grouped into categories

- The number of organizations reporting data for a particular category or cut: The number of organizations reporting data for a certain cut is an important indicator of the reliability of that data. If there are only a few data points, there is a significant chance that the data will not be representative. Ideally, we recommend using only using cuts with eight or more data points (we realize, however, that in some cases it may not be possible to find cuts of relevant data that include a large number of data points).

- Quartiles: Data are generally reported by quartile (see box page 54). Surveys commonly report three quartiles: the 25th percentile — the compensation amount above which 75 percent of all reported compensation data fall; the median or 50th percentile — the compensation amount above which 50 percent of all reported compensation data fall; and the third quartile or 75th percentile — the compensation amount above which 25 percent of all reported compensation data fall. Some surveys will also report the 10th percentile (90 percent of all data are higher), and the 90th percentile (10 percent of all data are higher).

- The date of the information presented: Surveys will show the effective date of the information they present.

BENEFITS AND TOTAL COMPENSATION INFORMATION

Some surveys will also report benefits and/or total compensation information. This can include

Fringe benefits: Some surveys will report fringe benefits paid, often by type of benefit such as health insurance or perquisites such as use of an automobile. These are not always quantified, and the survey may simply report the existence or prevalence of the benefit.

- Deferred compensation: Compensation that is accrued but will be paid after the calendar year in which it is earned. Deferred compensation is reported relatively rarely in standard surveys.

- Total compensation: If reported, this figure would include the cash value of all compensation, whether paid in the current year, deferred, or provided as a fringe benefit.

USING SURVEY DATA

Using survey data is something of an art; this is one area where the assistance of an experienced professional can be especially helpful. The goal is to use the survey "cut" that is as close as possible to the market the organization has identified as its own. The problem is that the data are presented in cuts representing discrete categories based on organizational characteristics, but these cuts do not necessarily take into account multiple characteristics. For example, an organization might see its marketplace as a social welfare organization in the Southwest, of budget size $5 million to $10 million, with 50 employees, and a chief executive with 10 years' experience. The published data may include each of these cuts, but not a cut of all the factors taken together (although, as noted, it is increasingly common to have access to the full database, making special cuts easier).

In some cases, the compensation committee may be able to purchase a special cut; if this is not possible, a simple approach is to take the single best cut. In the experience of the authors, budget size is the data cut most closely correlated, although by no means perfectly, with chief executive compensation. The next best cut is usually staff size. Adjustments for location or other factors may still be necessary if, for example, the organization is based in an area where compensation is significantly above or below the national average. Another approach is to approximate the marketplace by averaging, or "blending," the various data cuts that reflect aspects of the organization's marketplace. However, care should be taken with this approach, since some cuts may be "dominant" (if blending reduces, for example, a geographically based factor, an organization in New York or Los Angeles might find that it has set pay below market).

The committee must also decide which quartile or percentile of the marketplace is appropriate. Often, the committee will already have decided which quartile to use in determining the organization's desired position vis-à-vis the market. This determination should generally be reflected in the organization's compensation philosophy. The most common approach is to target the median of the marketplace.

Targeting the median or even a lower point is certainly the safest policy from a legal standpoint. An organization may choose to target above the median if the compensation committee can make a good case for the organization's need for special skills, experience, or leadership qualities. Such a case might exist in an organization that is repositioning itself, has ambitious growth plans, currently has an unusually skilled or experienced chief executive, or has a leading position within the community that justifies paying above the median of the market. However, targeting pay above the 75th percentile is unusual. Any organization targeting above the median should be able to explain its decision in writing; a target above the 75th percentile should have an especially strong justification.

The organization's market target does not necessarily dictate, however, which data cut to use. While an organization targeting the median will generally use median data, using a higher or lower quartile can be another approach to adjusting the data. For example, if an organization is substantially larger than the highest budget cut in a survey, the 75th percentile may be closer to the organization's market than the survey median. That is especially the case if the data demonstrate a reasonable correlation between scope (such as budget or staff size and compensation). In such a case, the compensation committee can use the 75th percentile on the grounds that it reflects the (unreported) median of *their* market. This adjustment method should be used with caution, but it might also be appropriate in cases where there are unusual factors that would differentiate the organization in question from the median organization in the survey.

HOW SALARY SURVEYS PRESENT AND ORGANIZE DATA

Salary surveys typically present the following information:

CHIEF EXECUTIVE OFFICER COMPENSATION AND BENEFITS

Data Presented in Thousands of Dollars	# ORG	BASE SALARY		
		25th Percentile	50th Percentile	75th Percentile
ALL ORGANIZATIONS	84	200.1	267.2	297.5
ORGANIZATIONS BY GEORGRAPHIC AREA				
Northeast	52	177.6	211.1	254.7
Southeast	7	164.9	199.1	211.5
Midwest	19	204.5	227.6	264.7
West	6	233.6	274.6	301.4
BUDGET SIZE				
Less than $25m	16	185.2	208.9	288.0
$25m to $50m	39	188.7	215.4	266.7
Equal to or greater than $50m	29	198.7	217.6	295.2
STAFF SIZE				
Less than 50	38	179.5	206.5	272.4
50 to 100	27	184.2	211.5	285.9
Greater than 100	19	199.7	214.4	302.4
ORGANIZATION TYPE				
Individual Member Association	35	211.4	237.8	299.8
Academic Institution	15	188.9	209.7	268.7
Museum or Cultural Institution	3	*	*	*
General Nonprofit	31	204.4	234.6	289.4

* Insufficent data

Total Cash Compensation			Benefits		
25th Percentile	50th Percentile	75th Percentile	25th Percentile	50th Percentile	75th Percentile
230.1	307.3	342.1	20.0	26.7	29.8
204.2	242.8	292.9	17.8	21.1	25.5
189.6	229.0	243.2	16.5	19.9	21.2
235.2	261.7	304.4	20.5	22.8	26.5
268.6	315.8	346.6	23.4	27.5	30.1
213.0	240.2	331.2	18.5	20.9	28.8
217.0	247.7	306.7	18.9	21.5	26.7
228.5	250.0	339.5	19.9	21.8	29.5
206.4	237.5	313.3	18.0	20.7	27.2
211.8	243.2	328.8	18.4	21.2	28.6
229.7	246.6	347.8	20.0	21.4	30.2
243.1	273.5	344.8	21.1	23.8	30.0
217.2	241.2	309.0	18.9	21.0	26.9
*	*	*	*	*	*
235.1	269.8	332.8	20.4	23.5	28.9

COMPENSATION FOR LONG-SERVING CHIEF EXECUTIVES

Compensation for long-serving chief executives is frequently greater than the median of the marketplace. However, this does not necessarily mean that compensation is excessive. Chief executives with a long tenure leading an organization tend to possess an especially deep knowledge of the organization and great skill at performing the responsibilities of the position. They typically receive a premium for their advanced skills and knowledge. Therefore, it may be appropriate to compensate a long-serving chief executive above the median of the marketplace. As always, compensation should not be so high as to violate legal standards. It would be appropriate, however, to compare pay for a long-serving chief executive to others in the same marketplace with comparable tenure and achievement. Because there is not always data available by tenure, one approach is to compare pay to the 75th percentile of the market for a chief executive with a long record of strong performance.

Compensation for a new or untested chief executive may be established below the median of the marketplace. Compensation would then be adjusted over time, as the chief executive demonstrates abilities and gains a greater understanding of the position.

One approach to tying compensation to performance and experience is to set compensation using a "salary range." This approach is described in detail in Chapter 8.

ADJUSTING THE DATA FOR INFLATION/MARKET MOVEMENT: "AGING" THE DATA

All surveys — and 990s — will report when the data were collected; the data must then be updated to the present to reflect the general increase of salaries in the marketplace since the data were collected. This is frequently referred to as "aging" the data. Market movement for salaries is similar, but not identical to, general inflation; even in a low or no inflation economy, salaries have historically moved upward (a severe economic contraction such as began in 2009 might be an exception — see the box on page 57). We recommend using survey data on salary movement in the market to determine an appropriate aging factor. Organizations publishing annual surveys include the Conference Board (www.conference-board.org) and WorldatWork. Several of the larger compensation consulting firms, such as Mercer Human Resource Consulting and Hewitt Associates, also produce regular surveys of market pay movement (see Suggested Resources for more information).

To age survey data, "raw" survey data (i.e., the data reported by the survey, not adjusted for subsequent market movement) is multiplied by an aging factor for each year, based on survey data published annually. Since the factor reported by the surveys reflects market salary movement for the entire year, it should be prorated if used with a survey that reports data midyear or if the committee wishes to set compensation effective midyear. Aging factors should also be prorated where unusual circumstances, such as the economic crisis beginning in 2008, cause a change in expected salary increases.

As an example, assume that the compensation committee is setting compensation for the chief executive to coincide with the beginning of its fiscal year on January 1, 2009. The committee would like to set compensation using a survey with data effective as of July 1, 2007.

According to published survey data, the median salary increase for nonprofit executives was 4 percent for all of 2007 and most of 2008. Salary increases fell to 0 percent after the onset of the financial crisis in October 2008.

Therefore, to age the survey data in the example, the committee would multiply the data by 2 percent for 2007 (reflecting the half year covered by the survey at a 4 percent annual rate), 3 percent for 2008 through October (reflecting a 4 percent annual factor for three-quarters of a year), and zero percent subsequently. Graphically, the formula would appear as:

$$(1+.04/12x6)x(1+.04/12x9)x(1+.00/12x3)$$

which simplifies to:

$$1.02x1.03x1=1.0506$$

In other words, to age the survey data to January 1, 2009, it should be increased by 5.06 percent.

AGING THE DATA IN A TIME OF ECONOMIC UNCERTAINTY

From the late 1990s through 2008, staff and management salaries in both the nonprofit and for-profit marketplaces increased at a remarkably consistent rate of between 3 percent and 4 percent a year. In many parts of the nonprofit sector, chief executive compensation rose at even faster rates. Most organizations financially able to adjust compensation followed average or median market practice. The stability of the data over time, and the fact that most organizations followed average practice, made the published survey data a reliable guide to market movement.

Published survey data on planned increases can become outdated, however, during severe economic conditions (recession or sharp inflation). Thus, as this book went to press in mid-2009, the country had entered a severe economic downturn, with the most recent survey data at least six months to a year old. In such circumstances survey data should be treated with extreme caution. Rather than using outdated information, organizations should talk to similar organizations in their community on how their compensation practice might be changing. Compensation consultants will also be familiar with up-to-date local trends. Some consulting firms may also conduct more up-to-date studies to reflect changes in the marketplace. For example, a number of firms conducted new studies after the September 11 terror attacks, and the authors' firm has surveyed its clients every six months since October 2008 in order to capture the most recent data on salary trends.

SPECIAL SURVEYS

One of the best ways of gathering data — probably the very best if the right set of organizations can be found — is to conduct a special survey. With the right participants, a special survey will provide up-to-date, quality controlled, and therefore more reliable data on organizations specifically chosen for their comparability. The IRS appears to favor this approach; its regulations specifically provide that smaller organizations (those with annual gross revenues of $1 million or less) may use compensation information from "three comparable organizations in the same or similar communities for similar services." Telephone calls are an acceptable way of gathering the information.[20]

However, some practical difficulties are involved in conducting a special survey:

- The organizations should be comparable in as many ways as possible, and identifying and securing the cooperation of a sufficient number of like organizations can be difficult.

- For the data to be statistically significant, the survey should include at least eight to 10 participants.

- Organizations are constantly being asked to participate in surveys, and harried HR staff may be inclined to say "no" to yet another request. It is important to explain the benefit to potential participants of accurate and up-to-date data specific to their marketplace.

- In certain sectors (health care, for example) antitrust issues may arise when organizations share compensation information. To minimize these, some authorities advise that the data be collected by an independent third party, that it be aggregated, and that at least five organizations participate in the survey.[21] Note, however, that where the data are publicly available on IRS Form 990s — as is the case with chief executive compensation — the potential for antitrust issues may be lessened.

With these caveats in mind, however, organizing a special survey can benefit all the participants, especially if the survey is conducted on a regular basis.

One of the authors' best-managed clients is a model for conducting a regular, focused survey of its marketplace.

- The board first develops a set of criteria for identifying comparable organizations:
  - Budget size
  - Comparable institutional focus (e.g., public policy, health, the arts)

---

[20] Internal Revenue Service, *Instructions for Form 990 2008,* pp. 66.

[21] Department of Justice and Federal Trade Commission, *Statements of Antitrust Enforcement Policy in Health Care* (Washington, DC: Government Printing Office, 1996); John Davis, *Salary Surveys and Antitrust: An Overview for the HR Professional* (Scottsdale, AZ: WorldatWork, 2003) notes that this guideline is generally accepted in industries other than health care.

- Diversity and nature of programs (multi-program vs. single focus)
- Scope (national in the case of this client)
- Number of locations
- Staff size
- Time in business

- Candidate organizations are then assessed in relationship to the criteria and a list of potential comparators created.
  - In the case of this organization, 49 organizations were invited to participate in the survey; 26 agreed to provide data.
- The survey was conducted and summary results shared with all participants.
- The survey is repeated every three years.

The following three examples illustrate different approaches to obtaining and using survey data.

Example 1: A Prominent Policy and Advocacy Organization

Based in Chicago, Organization X is one of the country's leading public policy and advocacy organizations with a high public profile. Organization X's chief executive must be both intimately familiar with the public policy issues on which the organization focuses, and capable of managing a large organization. Organization X must compete for top advocacy and management talent. It knows that general surveys will not be a sufficient source of data on these organizations.

Organization X wants the process for setting its chief executive's compensation to comply as closely as possible with IRS guidelines. The Compensation Committee is aware that, where possible, the IRS appears to favor custom surveys as a method for gathering market data. Furthermore, Organization X finds itself in a highly competitive marketplace. The Compensation Committee knows a custom survey is the best way to obtain up-to-date compensation data.

Since it possesses the financial resources to conduct a custom survey of its marketplace, the Compensation Committee decides to commission such a study. It examines the criteria that would help it identify comparable organizations, and develops a list of 15 of the largest public policy and other advocacy organizations with a national scope. It secures the participation of nine of these organizations and produces a survey with the data they report.

The survey serves as one source of market data for making the compensation decision. However, given the relatively small number of organizations that participated in the survey, the Compensation Committee supplements the survey data with data from the IRS Form 990 for all 15 organizations.

Finally, it adds data from a broader range of nonprofit organizations similar in size and complexity to Organization X, but with somewhat different missions. It obtains these data from a general survey of large nonprofit organizations. The survey is proprietary but Organization X obtains the data by promising to participate in the following year's survey.

The final compensation package for Organization X's chief executive is determined based on a blending of data from all three sources.

Example 2: A Small Regional Foundation

Foundation Y is a small foundation located in Memphis, Tennessee. It has a staff of three full-time employees — including the chief executive — and assets of $200 million. It does not have the financial resources to conduct a custom survey. The Council on Foundations (COF) Survey — a national published survey reporting data on foundations of all sizes — is the most specific source of survey data available. The COF Survey reports compensation data on chief executives with assets between $100 million and $250 million. However, the data include foundations in all regions of the country, which may have pay practices that differ from the mid-South region where Foundation Y is located. Furthermore, the Compensation Committee is aware that many of the chief executives of foundations within this asset range do not have full-time responsibilities.

One option for the foundation is to ask the Council on Foundations to do a special cut of its survey by both region and size — a service that they have typically supplied for COF members.

The foundation could also supplement the COF data with IRS Form 990 data from a group of foundations in Foundation Y's region with similar asset sizes and chief executives with similar responsibilities. The board identifies these organizations based on their local knowledge and personal experience. It carefully documents its criteria for establishing the comparator group, as well as the consistency of each comparator organization with the criteria.

The board uses the comparator group 990 data as the main source for pricing the chief executive, combined with the special COF cut if that is available or using the COF published data as an additional, supporting reference.

Example 3: A Medium-Sized Think Tank

Organization Z is a medium-sized think tank located in Washington, D.C. Given that there are relatively few think tanks, they can find no published surveys with specific data on think tanks.[22] Other published surveys do not accurately capture Organization Z's market.

---

[22] Since this is a fictional example, we have assumed a counter-factual. In fact there is a very good annual think tank survey, although it is restricted to participants only: AKRON, Inc. 2008 *Think Tank Compensation Survey.*

Through a contact at another think tank, the Compensation Committee is able to obtain a custom survey organized by the other think tank. However, the participants in the custom survey are all much larger than Organization Z. Therefore, the Compensation Committee identifies 10 think tanks that are roughly of equal size to Organization Z, and obtains compensation information from their IRS Form 990s. The think tanks do not focus on the same issues as Organization Z, but there are not enough think tanks of the same size, focusing on the same issues to constitute a distinct marketplace. This group of 10 think tanks is therefore the most appropriate marketplace for Organization Z. The data obtained from their Form 990s serve as the basis for determining the chief executive's compensation package.

Once the compensation committee has gathered sufficient data to meet the legal requirements and public expectations for understanding its target marketplace, it can move on to developing the elements of the organization's own compensation package. First, however, it should carefully review the legal standards for nonprofit chief executive compensation and ensure that the compensation level and structure it proposes will stand up to public scrutiny.

SUMMARY: ACTION STEPS FOR THE BOARD

- Before attempting to define the specific marketplace for the chief executive, the compensation committee should understand the differences between nonprofit and for-profit compensation practices, and the limitations placed on nonprofit compensation.

  o It should thoroughly understand the legal rules governing nonprofit compensation discussed in Chapter 6.

- The compensation committee's determination of the appropriate marketplace should be informed by the definition provided by the IRS in its intermediate sanctions regulations: "what would ordinarily be paid for like services by like enterprises under like circumstances."

- The compensation committee should then determine the specific marketplace for the chief executive based on a consideration of the criteria presented on page 46.

- Once the compensation committee has defined the marketplace, it should obtain sources of market data from among one or more of the following: IRS Form 990s of comparable organizations, published and proprietary surveys, and special surveys commissioned by the organization.

- The compensation committee must make sure it understands the data presented by these sources and uses it appropriately.

  o It must understand the appropriate "cut" of data, the percentile of data it wishes to target, and update ("age") the data for the movement of the salary market.

  o It may consider using a consultant to help it obtain and make use of data.

CHAPTER 6
MEETING THE LEGAL STANDARDS

Ensuring that the chief executive's compensation level and structure meet the legal standards set by the IRS for tax-exempt organizations is one of the board's most important responsibilities. If an organization does not adhere to these standards, the chief executive and its board members may be penalized. It is possible that the organization's tax exemption could be threatened. The board must also ensure that the organization follows state law, violation of which can also subject the organization and its leadership to penalties.

To ensure compliance, compensation committee members need first to understand the IRS's purpose in setting the standards and the definitions it uses in doing so. The IRS's purpose is to ensure that nonprofit organizations operate in ways that qualify them for tax exemption and to provide a legal guideline for making that determination. The standards apply to the types of organizations described in sections 501(a) and 501(c)(1)-(27) of the Internal Revenue Code (IRC), which the IRS terms tax-exempt or exempt organizations.

THE "PRIVATE INUREMENT" DOCTRINE APPLIES TO ALL NONPROFITS

All nonprofit organizations are subject to what is called the "private inurement" doctrine.

Simply put, private inurement is income or other financial gain from a nonprofit to an individual for which the nonprofit does not receive a comparable benefit in return (in other words, the value of the financial gain the individual receives from the organization exceeds the value of the services he or she provides to the organization). Persons engaging in private inurement are usually "insiders" who are in a position to divert nonprofit assets or income to their own benefit.

Federal tax law differentiates nonprofit organizations from for-profit organizations by forbidding nonprofits from engaging in private inurement. In the IRS's own words:

> [P]rivate inurement is likely to arise where the financial benefit represents a transfer of the organization's financial resources to an individual solely by virtue of the individual's relationship with the organization, and without regard to accomplishing exempt purposes.[23]

---

[23] IRS General Counsel Memorandum 38459, cited in Bruce Hopkins. *The Law of Intermediate Sanctions,* (New York: John Wiley & Sons, 2003), p. 24.

The private inurement doctrine does not forbid financial relationships between nonprofit organizations and insiders. Instead, it requires that the organization receive in return a benefit more or less equal to the financial gain to the insider.

The private inurement doctrine has three main implications for chief executive compensation at all tax-exempt organizations:

1. Compensation should be clearly tied to the chief executive's performance in leading the organization toward achievement of its mission ("accomplishing exempt purposes").

2. Compensation should be reasonable and not excessive.

3. Because there is no equity available in a nonprofit organization, compensation committees should be wary of any compensation arrangement that looks like the distribution of profits.

For IRC 501(c)(3) public charities and 501(c)(4) social welfare organizations, the private inurement doctrine is enforced through the "Intermediate Sanctions" regulations (see below). Private foundations and other organizations, such as 501(c)(6) associations, however, are not subject to the intermediate sanctions regulations. Private inurement still applies to them and in principle they — and other nonprofits not subject to intermediate sanctions — can lose their nonprofit status if they are found to be engaging in private inurement. Private foundations are also subject to the IRS's rules against self-dealing: transactions where someone who is in a fiduciary relationship with an organization acquires or makes use of property that belongs to the organization for his or her own benefit. The self-dealing rules completely forbid certain transactions — leasing of property, for example — between insiders and a private foundation, but do allow compensation of insiders, so long as it is not excessive and they do not act outside of their governance or staff roles.

Nonprofits other than 501(c)(3) public charities and 501(c)(4) social welfare organizations, are hence not subject to the intermediate sanctions regulations. They should nevertheless follow those regulations as much as possible (see box on page 71)

INTERMEDIATE SANCTIONS

The law introducing intermediate sanctions (IRC Section 4958) was enacted by Congress in 1996 in response to perceived abuses of nonprofit status. The sanctions are "intermediate" because they fall between revocation of tax-exempt status, the drastic but only penalty for abuse of the status before 1996, and no penalty at all. By providing for usable penalties, Congress hoped to strengthen IRS oversight of nonprofit organizations and their dealings with insiders.

The IRS intermediate sanctions regulations apply and define the private inurement doctrine for a subset of all nonprofits: IRC 501(c)(3) public charities and 501(c)(4) social welfare organizations. The IRS refers to these organizations as applicable tax-exempt organizations. The regulations penalize a disqualified person if he or she receives excess compensation from an applicable organization. A disqualified person is someone who is in a position to exercise substantial influence with respect to the organization's affairs. Disqualified persons include presidents, chief executives, chief operating officers, treasurers, chief financial officers, other key employees with substantial influence and decision-making authority, board members, close relatives of officers and board members, and others (such as founders) who are in a position to influence the organization.

To be in violation of the intermediate sanctions regulations (in other words, subject to the penalties described below), a transaction must meet a three-part test:

1. The organization involved must be an applicable tax-exempt organization: a 501(c)(3) public charity or a 501(c)(4) social welfare organization.

2. The transaction must involve a disqualified person.

3. An excess benefit transaction must have taken place. An excess benefit transaction is a form of private inurement; it is a "transaction in which an economic benefit is provided by an applicable tax-exempt organization, directly or indirectly, to or for the use of a disqualified person, and *the value of the economic benefit provided by the organization exceeds the value of the consideration* (including the performance of services) received for providing the benefit" [emphasis added].[24] In other words, it is a transaction in which the insider gets more from the nonprofit organization than the nonprofit receives in return.

If a transaction is judged to be in violation (see question above) of the intermediate sanctions, the IRS may impose penalties on both the individual disqualified person involved and on organization officials:

- The disqualified person owes a penalty of 25 percent of the excess benefit, that is, the amount found to be in excess of a reasonable benefit in exchange for the services provided. The person must correct (i.e., repay) the excess benefit within 90 days after the date of mailing of a notice of deficiency.[25] Failure to correct the excess benefit makes the disqualified person subject to a 200 percent penalty.

- Organization officials, including board members, chief executives, and officers, who "knowingly, willfully, and without reasonable cause" participate in an excess benefit transaction are subject to a 10 percent penalty with a total cap of $20,000 for all persons involved. The penalty is not imposed on the organization, but on the individuals themselves. In other words, board members are personally liable.

As a compensation committee develops its chief executive compensation package, it must pay close attention to the definitions and interpretations used by the IRS. The IRS defines compensation to include all economic benefits other than certain nontaxable fringe benefits and other small, technical categories, and uses a

[24] Internal Revenue Service, *Instructions for Form 990 2008.* p. 65; Bruce Hopkins, *The Law of Intermediate Sanctions* (New York: John Wiley & Sons, 2003), p. 100.

[25] IRC § 6212.

reasonableness standard in determining whether a particular compensation arrangement is an excess benefit. Reasonableness is defined as "the value that would ordinarily be paid for like services by like enterprises under like circumstances."[26] The legislative history of IRC Section 4958 and other commentary give some additional guidance on what is meant by reasonableness and therefore on what should be included in a compensation analysis to pass IRS muster. The criteria include

1. Compensation paid by similarly situated organizations, taxable and nontaxable, for functionally comparable positions

2. The need of the organization for the service of the individual being compensated

3. The relation of the individual's compensation to that of other employees in the organization

4. The individual's duties and performance history

5. The individual's prior compensation history

6. The location of the organization

7. Written offers from similar institutions for the services of the individual involved

8. Whether there was arm's length bargaining, that is, approval by an independent board or committee of the board

9. The individual's background, education, training, experience, and responsibilities

10. The size and complexity of the organization in terms of assets, income, and number of employees

11. The amount of time the individual devotes to the position[27]

Any analysis presented to the board should cover as many of the factors listed above as are applicable, and explain those factors in clearly understandable terms. None of the factors is dispositive by itself. In the experience of the authors, the most important factors to consider as part of a market analysis are the pay practices of similar organizations, the size and complexity of the organization, the pay practices in the organization's region or locality, and the duties of the employee. However, to date there is not enough experience with the IRS's application of the standards to understand which factors they consider in practice to be most important.

[p26] Internal Revenue Service, *Instructions for Form 990 2008*. p. 65-66.

[27] Bruce Hopkins, *The Law of Intermediate Sanctions* (New York: John Wiley & Sons. 2003), pp. 124–127.

REVENUE SHARING, INCENTIVES, AND BONUSES

Compensation arrangements that are at least in part based on the revenues of the organization are permissible under intermediate sanctions, as are incentives and bonuses, so long as their total amount is reasonable. (Although they are frowned on in some parts of the nonprofit world.) The IRS accepts that incentive plans can benefit a nonprofit organization, but the organization must receive proportionate benefit from incentive plans. Compensation committees should be especially careful in scrutinizing such arrangements and considering the maximum amount that might be earned. The committee may want to include a cap on compensation under such arrangements in order to ensure compliance with the law. The cap should be set using market comparisons to identify a reasonable total cash compensation level. In addition, compensation committees should be aware of the ethical and public image issues associated with paying the chief executive a percentage of the organization's total revenue. These issues are discussed further in Chapter 8.

Q **Is it common, or ethical, for the chief executive to receive incentive compensation based on fundraising revenues?**

A Revenue-based incentives are not common and are considered unethical by many nonprofits. The Association of Fundraising Professionals prohibits its members from receiving such compensation, and states that, where such compensation is percentage-based, "charitable mission can become secondary to self-gain" and "there is incentive for self-dealing to prevail over donors' best interests."[28] Donors may also feel such arrangements are unethical; therefore, organizations should be very cautious in linking fundraising to compensation. One way to avoid any possible appearance of unethical behavior is by having an organizational reach objective rather than an explicit fundraising objective. It is also good practice to make financial goals only one of several objectives; see the discussion in Chapter 2 on the balanced scorecard approach to objective setting.

From a legal standpoint, compensation arrangements that are at least in part based on the revenues of the organization are permissible under intermediate sanctions so long as their total amount is reasonable. Nevertheless, such arrangements are a red flag for intermediate sanctions purposes: The fact that they may lead to exceptionally large awards means that they may trigger special scrutiny from the IRS. Therefore, boards should consider the maximum amount that might be earned under such arrangements. The authors strongly recommend including a cap on compensation under such arrangements in order to ensure compliance with the law.

[28] Association of Fundraising Professionals, "Position Paper: Percentage-Based Compensation," www.Afpnet.org/tier3_cd.cfm?folder_id=899&content_itemid=1227 (accessed February 11, 2005).

A Sign-on bonuses are quite rare in the nonprofit world, but they are not unknown. As long as the total amount of compensation is not excessive, there should be no IRS concerns; moreover, if this is genuinely an arm's-length initial contract, it should be subject to the initial contract exception to the intermediate sanctions regulations. The authors know of no ethical bar to the suggested arrangement.

INITIAL CONTRACT EXCEPTION

An arm's-length contract negotiated for a new hire is exempt from intermediate sanctions, under the theory that the new hire is not a disqualified person because he or she does not yet have influence with the organization — arm's length negotiation is critical. This general principle has three modifiers:

1. There must be a written contract between the organization and the new chief executive that is executed before he or she is hired.

2. The exception applies only to fixed payments defined in the contract and not to contingent or discretionary payments. Accordingly, a bonus based on board discretion is not exempt from intermediate sanctions and will be judged by the usual reasonableness standard. A bonus that is based entirely on factors set in the initial contract, such as hitting certain preset revenue targets, is exempt, however.

3. There must be substantial performance from the person involved.[29]

THE REBUTTABLE PRESUMPTION OF REASONABLENESS

Congress, wanting to encourage boards to follow sound procedures in setting compensation, established guidelines on those procedures; if those guidelines are followed, there is a presumption that a compensation arrangement is reasonable. This rebuttable presumption of reasonableness shifts the burden of proof to the IRS in showing that an excess benefit transaction has taken place (that is, in rebutting the presumption). In order to fall under the rebuttable presumption of reasonableness, a compensation arrangement must meet three conditions[30]:

1. It must be approved in advance by an authorized body of the tax-exempt organization, composed entirely of individuals with no conflict of interest with respect to the compensation arrangement. This can include the governing body of the organization (i.e., its board), a committee of the governing body as allowed by state law, or other parties as allowed by state law.

[29] Internal Revenue Service. *Instructions for Form 990 2008.* p 66.

[30] Internal Revenue Service, Instructions for Form 990 2008, p. 66; Bruce Hopkins, *The Law of Intermediate Sanctions* (New York: John Wiley & Sons, 2003), p. 162.

2. The authorized body must obtain and rely on appropriate data as to comparability prior to making a determination. Data are appropriate if, "given the knowledge and expertise of the board's members, it has information sufficient to determine whether, under the valuation standards, the compensation arrangement in its entirety is reasonable or the property transfer at fair market value."[31] Appropriate sources and types of data are described in Chapter 5; the data must be presented in a way that allows a reasoned judgment on the part of the board, by showing how the criteria for reasonableness, such as compensation at organizations that are comparable in terms of mission, location, size, and complexity, have been applied. For organizations with $1 million or less in gross annual revenue, however, "appropriate comparability data includes data on compensation paid by three comparable organizations in the same or similar communities for similar services."[32]

3. The authorized body must adequately document the basis for its determination at the same time that the determination is made. This documentation must include

   a. the terms of the transaction

   b. the date

   c. the members of the body present during debate and those voting

   d. the comparability data obtained and relied on by the authorized body and how the data were obtained

   e. any actions by a member of the body with a conflict of interest

   f. documentation must take place within 60 days of the final actions or the next meeting of the body, whichever is later

   g. after documentation within 60 days, it must be approved by the authorized body within a "reasonable" time

The IRS urges nonprofits to comply as much as possible with the rebuttable presumption of reasonableness standards, even if they cannot fully meet the requirements, implying that even partial compliance will help in establishing the reasonableness of a compensation arrangement.[33] Satisfaction of the rebuttal presumption of reasonableness will also protect managers, including board members, from personal liability.

[31] Bruce Hopkins, *The Law of Intermediate Sanctions*, (New York: John Wiley & Sons. 2003), p. 165.

[32] Internal Revenue Service, *Instructions for Form 990 2008*, p. 66.

[33] Ibid.

A SECOND PROTECTION FROM PERSONAL LIABILITY

Beyond the rebuttable presumption of reasonableness, managers of nonprofit organizations have a second protection from personal liability under intermediate sanctions. Personal liability requires knowing participation in an excess benefit transaction; managers are held not to be knowing participants if they relied on a reasoned written opinion from a professional with respect to the elements of a transaction within the professional's expertise. The opinion must recite both the facts and the applicable standards. Professionals can include legal counsel with respect to the legal standards to be followed, but on compensation issues per se professionals are

> independent valuation experts who (1) hold themselves out to the public as appraisers or compensation consultants, (2) perform the relevant valuations on a regular basis, (3) are qualified to make valuations of the type of property or services involved, and (4) include in the written opinion a certification that the foregoing three requirements are met.[34]

An opinion from a compensation consultant will therefore give full protection to the board under the intermediate sanctions rules because board members will not "knowingly" approve excessive compensation. It will not protect the disqualified person absolutely from penalties but will still provide significant protection by supporting the "rebuttal presumption of reasonableness."

The organization itself does not face any penalties under intermediate sanctions but does have exposure under the private inurement prohibition, which could in theory lead to revocation of nonprofit status. An opinion from a compensation consultant will not give blanket protection against private inurement but it would be difficult for the IRS to revoke the tax exemption for an organization that set its compensation based on the opinion of a reputable consultant.

Summary: The intermediate sanctions regulations set up a clear three-step process for boards to follow to ensure compliance with the law:

1. Set up a formal process for setting compensation.

2. Obtain carefully researched comparable data on chief executive pay.

3. Document the decision-making process thoroughly.

The regulations seem complicated, but they should not be excessively burdensome if organizations are careful about following these three steps. Fundamentally, the intermediate sanctions regulations put into law a principle that any responsible board should already be following: paying the chief executive as much as necessary for the services provided, but no more than is justified by the market. The law sets out what is in fact a common-sense standard for defining the marketplace — a

---

[34] Bruce Hopkins, *The Law of Intermediate Sanctions,* (New York: John Wiley & Sons. 2003), p. 188.

standard more or less identical to the one the authors would recommend be used even in the absence of intermediate sanctions. In fact, those nonprofits that are not explicitly subject to intermediate sanctions face similar legal requirements and are well advised to act in accordance with the intermediate sanctions standards.

OTHER NONPROFITS AND "INTERMEDIATE SANCTIONS"

Our consulting firm is often asked about how foundations, trade associations, and other nonprofit organizations not formally subject to the intermediate sanctions regulations should manage compensation in light of IRS standards.

All nonprofits should follow the same steps as outlined for 501(c)(3) and (c)(4) organizations: Establish a formal process, obtain carefully researched comparable data, and document the decision-making process. Of course, the marketplace will differ according to the organization (trade association pay tends to be significantly higher than that for other nonprofits, for example). But the marketplace must still be researched and findings documented and formally considered.

While there is no formal protection for other nonprofits, adherence to intermediate sanctions safe-harbor procedures, even by organizations not subject to the regulations, is likely to provide some protection from the IRS.

As we have noted, all nonprofits are subject to the "private inurement" doctrine. As a result, they must ensure that compensation is "reasonable," "not excessive," and is clearly tied to the chief executive's performance in leading the organization toward achievement of its mission.

IRS FORM 990 REPORTING: A POSSIBLE TRAP FOR THE UNWARY?

Recall that the IRS requires almost all nonprofit organizations to file annual IRS Form 990 returns (the most prominent exceptions are certain religious and governmental organizations). (The new 990 form is discussed in detail in Appendix V). Among the items that must be reported are all fringe benefits, taxable or not

The requirement to report fringe benefits can be a trap for the unwary nonprofit because the IRS will treat unreported compensation as an "automatic" excess benefit transaction, even if it would otherwise be reasonable under the intermediate sanctions regulations. Thus, if an organization were to pay for spouse travel on a business trip, intending it as part of the compensation to the chief executive, but did not report the benefit on the organization's 990 or the individual's W-2 or Form 1099, and the individual did not report it on the individual income tax filing, the payment would automatically be considered an excess benefit transaction.[35]

---

[35] Lawrence M. Brauer and Leonard J. Henzke, Jr. "Automatic Excess Benefit Transactions Under IRC 4958." (www.irs.gov/pub/irs-tege.eotopice04.pdf.)

An organization that is subject to the intermediate sanctions regulations is also required to report any Section 4958 excess benefit transactions during the tax year, and any from past years of which it became aware.[36] The implication of this is that even though the intermediate sanctions penalties are paid by individuals, the organization can be harmed because it must publicly report and acknowledge involvement in a prohibited transaction.

COMPLYING WITH STATE LAW

When they are formed as nonprofit corporations under state law, nonprofits are subject to state, as well as federal, regulation and reporting requirements, and they have come under increasing scrutiny by state attorneys general in recent years. As a general rule, states follow the IRS regulations with respect to chief executive compensation, and a board that ensures compliance with federal regulations will meet state standards as well.

THE IMPORTANCE OF LEGAL COUNSEL

Given the increased level of scrutiny by both state and federal authorities and the increasing complexity of many nonprofit compensation plans, the authors recommend that organizations seek advice from experienced independent counsel when structuring both their decision-making process and their compensation plan. It is very important to make sure legal counsel is well versed in nonprofit compensation and tax law. It has been our experience that clients who have used counsel not experienced in these areas have not always received sound advice. Legal advice is especially important if compensation is complex or if it appears to be high by community standards or in comparison to past pay practices at the organization.

BOARD ROLE IN REVIEWING COMPENSATION FOR OTHER SENIOR STAFF

A nonprofit board has both a legal and fiduciary duty to review the compensation of senior staff below the level of the chief executive. While this has always been true, the new 990s will make it especially important that boards understand, review, and be prepared to defend senior staff compensation, which will now be reported in detail on the organization's Form 990.

Fiduciary duty. While the chief executive is generally responsible for hiring and setting the compensation of his or her staff, including senior staff members, the board is responsible for the organization's financial health and its mission success. The board should therefore review and approve the overall budget for compensation, including the compensation budget for senior staff. The board is also responsible (see Chapter 4) for setting the compensation philosophy of the organization. It should review the organization's compensation structure for its executives to ensure that it is consistent with the compensation philosophy.

[36] Internal Revenue Service, *Instructions for Form 990 2008*, p. 12; *Instructions for Schedule L (Form 990 and 990-EZ) 2008*.

The board generally will not (and should not) get involved in setting the specific pay levels for staff members, other than those classified as "disqualified persons" under the intermediate sanctions regulations. Staff pay in general is the chief executive's prerogative. The board should be comfortable, however, that the pay levels are adequate for hiring staff that can support the organization's mission and objectives, while at the same time not exceeding appropriate levels. The pay of officers of the organization will often require specific board approval.

Legal duties. The private inurement doctrine and intermediate sanctions regulations apply equally to all insiders and disqualified persons. It is important to keep in mind that disqualified persons include not just officers or other staff members "in a position to exercise substantial influence with respect to the organization's affairs," but also the relatives of such persons and hard-to-classify insiders, such as an organization's founder.

In the case of "intermediate sanctions," the board's liability is the same for all disqualified persons found to have received an excess benefit. Likewise, for all disqualified persons, the board must meet the three-part test described on pages 68–69 in order to qualify for the "rebuttable presumption of reasonableness." In effect, therefore, the board must review and specifically approve the compensation of all disqualified persons.

This is why, in our experience, it has become standard practice for boards to receive regular reports on the market compensation for both the chief executive and all possible disqualified persons. Boards choosing not to rely on an outside expert to provide this data should collect data themselves on all disqualified persons, or oversee the staff that assists in this process.

Public perception. With the new IRS Form 990, boards can no longer (if they ever could) plausibly claim ignorance of staff compensation. The new 990 requires nonprofit organizations to report whether a copy of the Form 990 was provided to the organization's governing body before it was filed and the process, if any, the organization uses to review the Form 990.[37] In other words, the IRS expects boards to have reviewed their organization's 990. Board members must therefore be sufficiently informed that they can be comfortable defending the compensation of every staff member appearing in the 990.

Comparing staff compensation to the market. The board (if the staff member is a disqualified person) or the organization (for remaining staff) should follow the same procedure for comparing staff compensation to the market as it does for the chief executive. It should

- Understand the nature of the position so it can be matched to appropriate market data.

- Identify sources of survey data (public, proprietary, and special surveys); 990 data may be used for executives and other highly paid employees, if enough data can be gathered.

---

[37] Internal Revenue Service, *Instructions for Form 990 2008,* p. 18.

- Determine the most appropriate cuts of survey data (type of organization, location, budget size, quartile).

- Determine a market price.

In many cases, the senior positions being directly reviewed by the board are likely to have clear market comparators (a chief financial officer is a chief financial officer). Some organizations may emphasize certain functions more than their peer organizations, or employees may have an unusual mix of responsibilities that makes comparison to to standard survey positions problematic. In those cases, it can be helpful to use "top paid" data in market pricing as well as direct market matches. "Top paid data" reports compensation information for positions of the same pay rank within an organization (e.g., second highest paid position). Organizing pay data by "top paid" reflects the fact that organizations value particular functions differently.

SUMMARY: ACTION STEPS FOR THE BOARD

- Ensure that the board understands the purpose of IRS rules governing nonprofit compensation.

- Understand the provisions of the "private inurement" doctrine and intermediate sanctions regulations.

- If the organization is subject to intermediate sanctions, ensure that the board understands the concepts of "disqualified persons" and "excess benefit" transaction.

- If the organization is subject to intermediate sanctions regulations, ensure that the board understands the penalties — including personal liability for board members — if a disqualified person is found to have received an excess benefit transaction.

- Understand the reasonableness standard set forth by the regulations for determining whether an excess benefit transaction has taken place.

- Understand how the "rebuttable presumption of reasonableness" and use of consultants can protect the board from liability for intermediate sanctions violations.

- Follow the steps that allow the board to take advantage of the "rebuttable presumption of reasonableness; these steps should be followed to ensure compliance with all rules regarding nonprofit compensation, regardless of whether the organization is subject to intermediate sanctions.

- Understand excess benefit transactions and 990 reporting requirements.

- Understand any applicable state laws regarding nonprofit compensation.

- Understand how intermediate sanctions and other rules apply to other senior staff, and take steps to ensure compliance.

CHAPTER 7

PASSING THE TEST OF PUBLIC AND STAKEHOLDER SCRUTINY

As strict as federal and state legal standards may be, an even more rigorous standard for judging chief executive pay is the test of public and stakeholder opinion. As Fisher Howe observes,

> The accountability of nonprofit organizations is principally to the public — a formless entity to which boards somehow owe a fiduciary answerability. In large measure, therefore, unless things go awry, boards and board members answer to their own consciences before the public and to their own self-determined principles of what is right and good.[38]

Boards must be fully prepared to explain and justify their organizations' chief executive (and senior staff) compensation packages to the media, the general public, and the organization's stakeholders. Not only is this information available in the public domain, it is the subject of public interest. The press is increasing the level of its investigative reporting on nonprofits, and reporters and others have access to the chief executive pay figures reported on each organization's IRS Form 990. These forms are increasingly available on the Web; many organizations post their own, and virtually all can be obtained through GuideStar (www.guidestar.org). And as we have discussed, the detail available on the 990 will soon be much greater than in the past, extending beyond cash compensation to such potentially sensitive items as perquisites (first-class travel, car services, and maid and chef services are undoubtedly rare in the nonprofit world, but boards providing them will no longer be able to claim they did not know what their chief executive was receiving).

Perceptions of pay practices are, of course, strongly influenced by the chief executive's experience, credentials, and performance; a long-serving chief executive who is universally recognized for strong performance faces different public expectations than an obscure and untested new hire. No matter what the chief executive's background, however, the compensation package will potentially face the front page test: How comfortable will board members be if every detail of the chief executive's pay package is published on the front page of the local newspaper? In the case of larger nonprofits, how comfortable will board members be if their organization appears in the Chronicle of Philanthropy's annual issue on the top compensated chief executives in the nonprofit world — or if the front page in question is that of *The New York Times, The Wall Street Journal,* or *The Washington Post?*

[38] Fisher Howe, *The Nonprofit Leadership Team,* (San Francisco: Jossey-Bass, 2004), p. 154.

In setting chief executive compensation, the compensation committee must be especially sensitive to the perceptions and expectations of those most likely to take an interest in the organization's pay practices, including donors, volunteers, and the organization's staff. Donors seek assurance that their money is being used wisely and effectively. Volunteers need to believe that they are giving their time to a worthy organization. Members of both groups may perceive apparently high pay levels as diversions of funds that could or should be going to the organization's mission. These stakeholders may also have expectations based on the mission and history of the organization; some types of nonprofits, such as advocacy organizations, groups working with the poor or underprivileged, and groups with a religious affiliation or origin, may be expected by supporters, staff, and the public to pay more modestly.

Stakeholders are particularly sensitive to mixed signals transmitted by the compensation committee or the board, especially when the board's words send one message and its actions send another. An example comes from the United Way of the National Capital Area, which hired Charles Anderson as its executive director in early 2003. Anderson succeeded interim director Robert Egger, who had taken a much-below-market salary of $85,000 during his tenure. In August 2004, according to *The Washington Post*, "the board of directors quietly voted [Anderson] a $25,000 raise, on top of his $190,000 annual salary.... Even those who approved of the raise said the decision should have been announced. 'We were going to be a transparent organization,' said Harriet Guttenberg, former chairman of the Montgomery United Way advisory council." In fact, the board had justification for the raise: "board member John T. Schwieters said Anderson was underpaid compared with chief executives of other United Ways and local nonprofits of similar size. 'I thought it was important to recognize the stress and strain he's been under…and bring him up to the level of other people,' Schwieters said."[39] However, many of the organization's stakeholders felt that this reasoning had not been conveyed before the raise was announced. If the board had acted in accordance with its stated goal of transparency, it might have averted much of the negative feeling that the raise engendered among its key stakeholders.

INTERNAL STAKEHOLDERS: THE STAFF

Organization staff members are a pivotal stakeholder group, and the compensation committee must consider the organization's current compensation structure for all of its employees when developing the chief executive's compensation package. Compensation sends a powerful message to staff about the board's priorities for the organization and its regard for the employees who carry out the organization's mission.

The compensation committee should be able to demonstrate that the chief executive compensation package is part of a coherent overall pay system, based on the market place for each position, and reflecting appropriately the skill and experience of both

---

[39] Jacqueline L. Salmon, "United Way Chief Toils to Resuscitate Charity," *The Washington Post*, November 1, 2004.

the chief executive and the nonprofit's staff. A coherent, defensible system tells employees that the entire staff is part of a team and that the committee takes seriously its accountability to all of the organization's stakeholders. When the compensation committee allows a major disparity between chief executive compensation and the compensation structure for other staff, it may send the message to employees that it thinks the chief executive is crucial to realization of the organization's mission, and staff members are relatively unimportant.

Staff members expect that the chief executive's pay will be broadly consistent with the pay levels and compensation structure for the rest of the organization and with the chief executive compensation offered in the past. Broadly consistent does not mean identical; it means logical given the existing compensation structure and the culture of the organization. The chief executive's pay will in almost all cases be higher than that of other employees, but it should not usually be disproportionately higher. (Common exceptions: Athletic coaches and professors of medicine are paid more than the president at some universities. Persons in revenue-generating positions at some nonprofits can also earn more than the chief executive, at least in good years.)

In the authors' experience, the chief executive salary is set at most 60 to 70 percent above that of the next highest paid employee. Some organizations are also considering putting chief executive pay a level no higher than a certain multiple of average pay in the organization, or of the pay of the lowest paid staff member. A 2007 survey by the authors found that chief executive pay was typically five to six times that of the lowest paid employee in many nonprofits.

There are, however, exceptions that may be based on the particular circumstance of an organization. One exception is found in some trade associations, where the differential in pay may be very large. Another example may be found when an organization is very small, for instance a nonprofit that has only a chief executive position and several administrative support positions on its staff.

Boards also need to bear in mind that chief executives can be paid too little in comparison to their staff. Chief executive pay that is much below market may compress pay for senior staff. This can result in poor morale and the loss of key employees.

The chief executive compensation package may also include elements that are not made available to other employees, such as a bonus or incentive; or bonus or incentive pay may be set at higher levels for the chief executive than for other staff. Chief executives and other highly compensated employees may have certain perquisites or benefits not available to other staff, including deferred compensation or special retirement arrangements. Again, however, these should not be so large as to be inconsistent with the organization's culture and practices or with the expectations of the local community. Of course, the total package must be consistent with the marketplace to meet legal standards.

RED FLAGS

Certain forms of compensation are "red flags" even if they are reasonable from a purely legal perspective (i.e., total compensation, including the cash value of bonuses, deferred compensation, and perquisites, is consistent with market practice). The most common red flags are bonuses or incentives and perquisites that appear excessive or lavish. Thus, while bonuses are acceptable practice in the nonprofit sector, the level of bonuses is far below those in some parts of the for-profit sector. Outside the trade association marketplace, bonuses or incentives greater than 25 percent of base pay are rare; standard practice, among organizations offering them, is for bonuses at the median to be in the 10 percent to 15 percent range, with some paying as little as 5 percent and a few as high as 30 percent. Boards should be especially careful about large, ad hoc bonuses that are not part of a pre-established compensation plan with clear objectives.

Perquisites may legally be provided (again subject to the market test for overall compensation), but may be inappropriate for the organization's culture. "Luxury" perquisites — a personal chef, frequent first-class air travel, trips to exotic places — will almost always risk negative press attention and public reaction, even if there is a business rationale and the total cost of the perquisites is not that large. If boards want to reward a chief executive, they are better off paying somewhat higher cash compensation, (again, consistent with market practice) than providing perquisites that may appear inappropriate to the public.

Two recent cases illustrate the dangers of approving perquisites or expenses that may be perceived as lavish or excessive. In 2007, the secretary of the Smithsonian was forced to resign after the details of a federal audit found that he had charged $2 million in expenses over six years for items including furniture and maintenance for his office and residence. The Smithsonian's board had authorized these expenses as reasonable under the terms of his contract, and initially did not take action based on the audit. However, details of the audit were obtained and published by the *Washington Post*, causing a public scandal which forced the Secretary to resign.[40] Similarly, in 2005, the president of American University was removed by the board of trustees after it was reported that he had been charging the university for lavish personal expenditures. Though the details were in dispute, the board, with pressure from students and faculty (which returned a vote of no confidence), quickly voted to remove the president.[41] Both cases illustrate the point that boards should be extremely cautious about approving payments that, while they may seem reasonable to the board, run the risk of negative reaction from other stakeholders.

[40] James V. Grimaldi, "Smithsonian Documents Detail Chief's Expenses," *The Washington Post* Online, March 19, 2007, www.washingtonpost.com/wp-dyn/content/article/2007/03/18/AR2007031801369.html.

[41] Susan Kinzie and Valerie Strauss, "Trustees Oust AU's Ladner as President," *The Washington Post* Online, October 11, 2005, www.washingtonpost.com/wp-dyn/content/article/2005/10/10/AR2005101000808.html.

HOW WILL THE PUBLIC REACT?

Meeting the test of public scrutiny means being accountable to donors, staff, and the public. However, when developing its chief executive compensation package, the compensation committee needs to go beyond acting out of self-preservation. The committee's goal should be not merely to develop a package that it can defend against legal scrutiny and public questioning, but to take advantage of the opportunity to make a positive statement about the organization.

This is where the work that the compensation committee has done in reviewing the organization's mission, priorities, and objectives becomes an asset. A compensation committee that can set its organization's chief executive compensation package in the context of the organization's vision for the future and the outcomes that it hopes to achieve, is in a good position to make a positive public impression, and it need not be hesitant to announce the compensation terms once the new chief executive is hired.

The best way of judging potential public reaction to chief executive compensation is for compensation committee members to use their own experience with the organization and the community to predict how the package they are planning will be perceived.

In our opinion, the board should have no reticence about making its compensation decision fully public before it appears on the 990 form. A commitment to this level of candor helps an organization maintain its integrity, because it ensures that the board will ask itself about public reaction to its compensation practices. Taking the test of public scrutiny seriously has another advantage as well: A compensation package that is acceptable to the public is almost certain to also pass legal muster.

QUESTIONS ON PUBLIC PERCEPTION FOR COMPENSATION COMMITTEE MEMBERS

Committee members should ask themselves the following questions:

- What would my reaction be, as a member of the community, if a comparable local nonprofit compensated its chief executive at the proposed level? If it provided the same level of bonus or types of perquisites?

- What is the history and nature of this nonprofit, and what constraints might that put on pay?

- What expectations do staff members have about the chief executive's pay level? How will the staff react to this pay package? How does the pay of high-achieving staff members compare with the proposed chief executive pay? How would I react if I were one of those staff people?

- Is there any reason to think that the organization may be under press scrutiny for any of its practices aside from chief executive pay? Do we have a process for responding to inquiries from the press or the public?

- How is the chief executive perceived, or likely to be perceived? If the chief executive's compensation were questioned, what credentials or performance record would I as a board member point to in order to justify the proposed compensation?

- How can I as a board member explain the chief executive's compensation in relation to the organization's mission, priorities, and objectives?

- How comfortable would I as a board member be in publicizing the proposed compensation arrangement? How comfortable do I think the chief executive would be?

SETTING PAY IN DIFFICULT TIMES

Setting compensation to meet public and stakeholder expectations is especially important when the organization is experiencing financial stress, or when the overall economy is weak. In those situations, it must be clear that the chief executive and senior staff are sharing the burden of pay restraint and cost cutting. If pay cuts are being made, the chief executive should take the lead, along with executive staff; if salaries are frozen or salary increases are below-market, the highest level staff should again demonstrate how their compensation is affected at least as much — and ideally more — than lower level staff. That is how one prominent client of the authors responded to the 2008/09 economic crisis with a pay freeze for the chief executive, but a modest 2 percent increase for staff (consistent with the most recent survey data). In an organization where the chief executive's compensation is highly dependent on incentive compensation, his or her base salary might be adjusted in line with other staff, but the organization would cut or forgo incentive pay. Again, what is important is that chief executive pay not be seen as rising faster than that of other staff during a financially difficult period.

TEST CASE: "WE ARE ON THE *CHRONICLE OF PHILANTHROPY* TOP EARNER LIST — NOW WHAT?"

Every year the *Chronicle of Philanthropy* publishes a special issue on nonprofit compensation — with a list of the top earners among charities and foundations.[42] Appearance on the *Chronicle* list is likely to generate attention — from others in the press, from donors, and from the public. There is no reason to panic if the board has followed the advice outlined in this chapter. First, the board should know before the *Chronicle* list appears that the organization is likely to be listed and will have made its compensation decision in full recognition of that fact. All board members should be aware of this possibility because they will have reviewed the organization's 990 and will have been briefed by the compensation committee on the market comparability data gathered for "intermediate sanctions" purposes. The comparability data will have shown that the organization is paying its chief executive at a certain level of the nonprofit marketplace. If that happens to be at the higher end of the marketplace and the board believes that level is appropriate, it needs to be prepared to explain why. Second, the board should have carefully determined the nature and level of compensation, so that the organization can confidently justify and defend its compensation decisions. Third, the organization should have already been transparent and forthcoming about its pay practices with the relevant stakeholders, so that the information in the *Chronicle* article comes as no surprise to any of its key constituencies. Press (especially local press), key donors and supporters, and any other important stakeholders should have been briefed beforehand on chief executive compensation.

---

[42] Noelle Barton and Ben Gose, "Executive Pay Outpaces Inflation," *Chronicle of Philanthropy,* October 2, 2008.

SUMMARY: ACTION STEPS FOR THE BOARD

- The board should be fully aware of and prepared to defend the compensation package for the chief executive.

  - We recommend that an organization make a commitment from the outset to disclose the chief executive's compensation before it is made publicly available on the organization's 990; this ensures that the board will make a decision in keeping with the organization's mission, culture and the expectations of all shareholders.

  - The board should approach public disclosure of compensation in terms of making a positive statement about how the compensation package will help the organization achieve its objectives; if the board has followed the advice presented in Chapters 2 and 3, it should feel comfortable announcing the compensation package.

- The board should understand that the compensation received by nonprofit executives is easily available to both press and public, and the subject of public and media interest.

  - Board members should draw on their own experience in predicting how the compensation package will be received by the public.

- The board should consider the various stakeholder groups, and the effect of the chief executive's compensation on how these groups view and contribute to the organization.

  - Be aware that certain groups with vested interests in the organization — such as donors — may have especially strong reactions to the chief executive's compensation, which in turn may have a significant impact on the functioning of the organization.

  - Chief executive compensation which is set without communicating a clear rationale, or which is far above compensation for other staff may give the impression that the contributions of staff are not adequately valued.

  - The board should be able to demonstrate that the chief executive's compensation is part of an overall compensation system where all staff are paid based on the marketplace for their position and their skills and experience.

  - Perquisites received only by the chief executive and/or other senior staff may be seen as excessive, depending on the amount and the organization's mission and culture; the board should be aware of any such "red flags."

CHAPTER 8

UNDERSTANDING THE ELEMENTS OF COMPENSATION

We now come to the heart of the matter: establishing the appropriate salary level and compensation plan for the chief executive. By the time the compensation committee has reached this stage, it will have worked through the series of steps outlined in the preceding chapters in order to ensure that its compensation decisions meet the tests of legal and public scrutiny:

- Establishing a process for setting executive compensation

- Reviewing the organization's mission, priorities, and objectives and the chief executive's role in achieving them

- Establishing a compensation philosophy

- Developing a title, job description, and profile for the chief executive

- Reviewing the organization's marketplace and learning what level of compensation is consistent with it

- Understanding the legal constraints on chief executive compensation and on the board process for setting it, especially the private inurement doctrine and the IRS intermediate sanctions regulations

- Understanding the constraints that the nature and history of the organization, and any public or other stakeholder concerns, might place on chief executive compensation, and the opportunity that chief executive compensation presents for sending a message about the organization's mission and priorities

The compensation committee must now decide how it wants to structure the chief executive compensation package. The elements of a compensation package are base salary; extra cash compensation, such as bonus or incentive awards; retirement and savings plans; deferred compensation; sign-on and retention bonuses; and other benefits and perquisites. The compensation committee must identify the elements that it wishes to incorporate and those that it cannot or will not include. It must also identify the parameters beyond which it cannot or will not go in terms of total compensation value and each element of compensation before deciding on a proposed compensation plan. Finally, the board should consider how it will assess annual performance and award bonuses and incentives, if those are part of the compensation package. It also must determine if base salary will be stable through the life of a contract or if the base salary will be adjusted annually based on both performance and changes in the marketplace (annual adjustments are a common feature of executive compensation plans). If pay is subject to adjustment, the board should identify the kind of data it will use in making those adjustments and the process for adjustment.

Q My board chair and I would like to know what is common practice, or what options exist, for building in merit raises/bonuses for chief executive contracts. How do other nonprofits handle this? Is it put in the contract? Is it tied to performance?

A It is not uncommon for chief executive contracts to include guidelines for merit raises and/or bonuses. The contracts will generally either provide a mechanism for adjusting pay or provide for regular increases or bonuses at board discretion. Pay might, for example, increase annually by the salary movement in your area as reported by an authoritative survey source. Incentives could be linked to the achievement of certain objectives, or to the chief executive's remaining on the job for a certain number of years.

Even when the mechanism for adjusting salaries and providing bonuses is included in a contract, the board usually retains some discretion in adjusting the amount awarded on the basis of performance and/or the organization's financial status. We believe it is important for boards to be able to adjust compensation to reflect performance and the financial condition of the organization, and strongly recommend that adjustments not be completely automatic. Contracts with incentives will often specify the incentive amount but leave it to the board to establish organizational goals and assess the chief executive on the attainment of those goals.

We recommend that performance be awarded annually through a formal board review that includes preset performance objectives. Salary should be adjusted based on inflation/market movement and performance. Any incentive earned should be based on performance.

Please see the discussion on page 94 for best practices on designing a performance management system to decide merit increases and incentive plans.

As the board considers the structure of the compensation and benefits package, it must keep in mind its total value. Total compensation is the standard for passing the legal tests. Total compensation is also important in meeting the test of public scrutiny (although, as we have discussed, particular elements of compensation, such as bonuses and perquisites, also need to be examined carefully).

BASE SALARY AND ANNUAL SALARY ADJUSTMENTS

Base salary is defined as annual compensation exclusive of all one-time or contingent payments. Base salary is the one element common to all compensation packages, and makes up the lion's share of total compensation in almost all nonprofit compensation packages. In fact, for the majority of nonprofits, base salary is likely to be the only compensation element other than benefits. It is thus especially important that base salary be set appropriately.

Research on the organization's marketplace will have given the compensation committee an idea of the typical base salary for chief executives at comparable organizations; review of the organization's culture, its compensation history for chief executives and other staff, and its current financial picture will have helped the committee determine whether matching market norms is feasible (and desirable). This information taken together enables the compensation committee to set a target base salary amount and a range within which it is willing and able to negotiate with a chief executive candidate.

ANNUAL SALARY INCREASES WHEN THE ECONOMY IS WEAK

As we have noted elsewhere, from the late 1990s through 2008, salaries in both the nonprofit and for-profit marketplaces increased at a remarkably consistent rate. However, in periods of economic turmoil — like the one beginning in late 2008 — boards need to exercise special care in understanding both the market and the ability of their organization to adjust compensation. Salaries in the marketplace may increase at a slower rate than projected before the onset of a period of economic instability, and may fluctuate with changing economic conditions. As of the writing of this book, for instance, a survey of over 200 nonprofit organizations conducted by Quatt Associates found that the majority of nonprofits were either freezing or sharply reducing base salary increases for the coming year.[43] The survey also found that incentive awards were decreasing in many cases.

During such periods of instability, boards should therefore examine the most recent available data on market movement. Adjustments to chief executive salary may also be constrained by the organization's financial circumstances. Even if an organization can afford to increase the chief executive's salary, if it is reducing planned salary increases for staff due to budgetary reasons, the board should weigh carefully a decision to increase the executive's salary in excess of the increase given to staff. Some organizations are considering an increased reliance on incentive compensation to control the fixed costs associated with base salaries. Such "at-risk plans" can provide a competitive total cash compensation opportunity while at the same time managing base salary costs. As discussed earlier, the advantages of such plans may need to be explained to stakeholders. In addition to a more conservative approach to cash compensation, organizations are also looking critically at their benefits package and its affordability. Some have responded by increasing the health care contributions required from employees, and reducing the organizational contribution to the retirement plans.

Boards need to be aware, however, that bad times will eventually end — and that they may then find themselves playing catch-up if their organization has held compensation below market.

---

[43] Quatt Associates, *March 2009 Salary Planning Survey.*

The base salary amount will also depend on whether the organization chooses to include a bonus or incentive element. In looking at the marketplace, the organization should compare the proposed total cash compensation for the chief executive (base salary plus bonus or incentive) to market total cash for its marketplace. An organization may choose to offer a higher base salary and no bonus or incentive, or a lower base salary with a bonus or incentive; but in either case the total package should be benchmarked against market total cash for the organization's marketplace.

One common way to set the base salary is to place it within a market-based salary range. Salary ranges are a very common method for managing staff compensation. They are less common for chief executives, whose compensation is often managed closer to market. If the board decides to use a salary range for its chief executive, a common model extends from 80 percent to 120 percent of the center of the salary range (often set at the market median). With a long record of outstanding performance, pay may go up to as much as 110 percent or 120 percent above the target. Thus, if the organization has determined from its research that the median of the marketplace is $100,000, the salary range based on this median would go from $80,000 to $120,000 with salaries at the higher end of the range being contingent upon long service and demonstrated mastery of the position.

Even if the position is within a market-based range, it is important to regularly test the salary against the marketplace. First, the market target (and hence the entire range) should move annually based on market movement. Second, if compensation is set substantially above the center of the range (at, say 110 percent or 120 percent of the center of the range), the organization should not simply assume that compensation is consistent with the marketplace because it is within a standard range. It should compare the proposed compensation directly to market. This is even more important for an organization paying above the median of the marketplace (for example, at the 75th percentile of the market). We often find, therefore, that organizations targeting the 75th percentile of the marketplace have a policy of not going more than a certain amount above their target (no more than 5 percent above, for example, or to 105 percent of the target range).

Please also note that in this model initial salary is not necessarily at the center or target of a salary range. In fact, standard compensation practice is to pay new employees somewhat below the center of the base salary range so that they move up through the range as they receive annual merit pay increases. Salary above the market range (at 105 percent or more of the market, as a rule of thumb) should be defensible relative to the demonstrated competence, performance, and other characteristics of the person holding the position. However, a compensation committee can also use the salary range to recognize the experience and past performance levels of stronger chief executive candidates by dividing the range into three segments.

MINIMUM	TARGET RANGE		MAXIMUM
20 Percent Below Target	5 Percent Below Market	5 Percent Above Market	20 Percent Above Target
DEVELOPMENTAL	**FULL PERFORMANCE AND EXPERIENCE**		**OUTSTANDING**

Many chief executive candidates will likely have skills and competencies that are fully developed and will have performed consistently in positions of responsibility in the past. Base pay for these strong candidates could be set from 5 percent below to 5 percent above market. For a chief executive candidate whose skills and competencies are still developing, the compensation committee might offer a base salary that is as much as 10 percent or 20 percent below the target. For a chief executive candidate whose background and experience are exceptional, the compensation committee might offer a base salary that is above the target, although this allows less room for future salary growth. Again, if much above the target of the range, be sure that the amount is defensible in terms of its market position.

Annual Salary Adjustments

In addition to setting base pay, the compensation committee must determine how annual salary adjustments will be made. Nonprofit organizations often adjust the chief executive's salary annually to reflect both performance and movement in the marketplace. Market movement for salaries is similar, but not identical to, general inflation; even in a low or no inflation economy, salaries have historically moved upward (a severe economic contraction such as began in 2008 might be an exception — see the box on page 85). It is thus important to obtain data specifically on salary trends in the organization's marketplace, and not to depend on inflation data such as the Consumer Price Index to determine an appropriate salary adjustment. Organizations compiling such data include WorldatWork, the Conference Board, Quatt Associates, and several of the large human resources consulting firms (see Suggested Resources for a comprehensive list).

Linking Pay Adjustments to Performance

Salary adjustments should also be tied to the chief executive's performance. We recommend that boards review performance annually. The central function of the performance review is to help the chief executive build on recognized strengths and improve performance in identified areas of need. We recommend that the performance review be based on a combination of previously determined performance goals and a review of the executive's achievements and leadership throughout the year. The goals can be a combination of institutional goals based on the organization's mission, critical objectives, strategic plan, if one exists, and/or annual operating business plan, and individual goals or leadership achievements specific to the chief executive (the "balanced scorecard" planning discussed earlier can be helpful here).

With today's strict public and legal scrutiny of executive pay practices, the performance review also serves another key function. Tying executive compensation levels, salary adjustments, and any extra cash payments to the performance review has the desirable outcome of demonstrating a solid rationale for executive compensation levels and decisions.

The best way to link compensation to performance is to decide on the performance review process *before* the executive performance evaluation takes place. The performance criteria and the link between compensation decisions and the performance assessment should also be specified in advance. We recommend that the process be formalized as part of the organization's annual governance process. As part of this process, the chief executive and the board would work together annually to establish the goals for the organization and their link to compensation.

The governance process should also define in writing how the board or compensation committee will communicate its performance assessment and any change in compensation to the chief executive. For example, the board could agree with the chief executive that achieving stated objectives would mean (finances allowing) a certain percentage increase in salary, or the award of an incentive amount. Going beyond the objectives would be worth more.

In the absence of a previously established link between pay and performance, the next best thing is to decide on an appropriate reward (a salary increase, an ad hoc bonus, or some combination of the two, consistent with market total compensation) and carefully explain to the chief executive the particular achievements that justify the increase or bonus. That explanation could then serve as the basis for the following year's performance plan. In the experience of the authors, less formal and predictable approaches can lead to disappointment and strained relations when board and executive expectations are inconsistent. The board may feel it is giving a handsome increase; the chief executive may have expected more based on his or her perception of performance. Establishing expectations beforehand can avoid this.

A market-based salary range provides a way to determine appropriate increments for base salary adjustments. Individual increases within the salary range depend on two factors: position in range (i.e., vis-à-vis the market) and performance. All other things being equal, persons low in the range receive larger increases because they are further below the market, and persons with stronger performance receive larger increases than weaker performers. Thus a person whose salary was below the midpoint in year 1, and whose performance was excellent, would receive an increase that moves base salary closer to the midpoint (i.e., an amount substantially larger than just the movement of the range). On the other hand, a person whose salary was above the midpoint, and whose performance was excellent, would receive a smaller increase than the person below the midpoint with equal performance (still above market movement alone probably, but only modestly more).

(For more information on the evaluation process, please see "Best Practices for Designing a Performance Management Plan" on page 94.)

BONUSES, INCENTIVES, AND OTHER ANNUAL CASH COMPENSATION AWARDS

After base salary, the next most common element in chief executive compensation is some type of extra cash compensation in the form of an annual bonus or incentive. While the terms are often used interchangeably, a bonus usually refers to an amount award at the discretion of the board based on its judgment of performance at the end of a performance cycle, while an incentive is an annual cash amount that has been established at the beginning of a performance cycle for a specified level of performance. It is therefore an "incentive" to accomplish agreed on goals and/or leadership behaviors.

The inclusion of extra cash compensation for chief executives is becoming increasingly common among nonprofit organizations. It is more common among larger organizations, and is seen most often in health care–related organizations, trade and other business associations, professional societies, public media organizations, and other nonprofits that may compete for talent with the for-profit sector. It is becoming more common, too, among academic institutions. Extra cash compensation for chief executives is less common among foundations and advocacy organizations. Interest across the nonprofit sector has been growing, however, as a way to control fixed salary costs in difficult times, while still motivating and retaining strong performers

As noted earlier (see page 6), estimates of the percentage of nonprofits with chief executive bonus or incentive programs vary depending on the survey, and the specific segment of the nonprofit sector. Nevertheless, they are clearly acceptable practice and common especially among larger nonprofits.

If offered, bonuses and incentives are generally paid annually, but they can also be structured over a longer term, with payment delayed for more than a year. Long-term incentives are used to encourage retention (the incentive is paid after a specified number of years to encourage the chief executive to stay with the organization), for the achievement of multiyear objectives (e.g., the achievement of an ambitious mission, development, or growth objective), or both.

A compensation committee may choose to pay part of a chief executive's total compensation in the form of a bonus or incentive for several reasons:

- **Recognition of achievement:** Boards often like to have the ability to recognize extraordinary achievement by providing a bonus. The bonus might be awarded at the end of a successful year, or upon achieving an important organizational objective. Boards need to be careful in how they award ad hoc bonuses, however. The amount paid must be consistent with organizational and community expectations and legal standards. Even an ad hoc bonus should still be tied to identifiable achievements whether seen in observable results or demonstrated leadership; otherwise, there is a risk that the bonus will simply become an entitlement. A bonus that is not tied to particular achievements is also less motivating, since it is not clear what behavior or successes are being rewarded.

- **Performance focus and motivation:** Extra cash compensation plans can be used to identify key objectives and encourage chief executive and organizational performance. In such plans, the accomplishment of key objectives is rewarded with incentive pay. The purpose of incentive-linked performance plans, it must be emphasized, is not to make the chief executive work harder (almost all chief executives work hard); it is to make sure he or she focuses on the main objectives of the organization and shows desired qualities of leadership and adaptability to unforeseen challenges.

- **Market competitiveness:** Especially with larger nonprofits, or with chief executives coming from the for-profit sector, market-based expectations for a bonus opportunity may exist.

- **Management of compensation costs:** An incentive or bonus is a way to align total chief executive compensation with the market without committing the organization to paying the full amount in fixed base salary. In a bad year the organization can cut or forgo the bonus without having to reduce base salary. Annual salary increases can also be more moderate, reducing fixed costs over the long run.

Bonus and incentive amounts at nonprofits are relatively modest by the standards of for-profit organizations. Quatt's 2008 survey of pay practices at large nonprofits found that among those organizations providing their chief executive with a bonus, the middle 50 percent (from the 25th percentile to 75th percentile) of bonuses as a percentage of salary was 13 percent to 31 percent. Another survey, which reports pay practices for both large and small nonprofits, found that the median chief executive bonus was 10 percent of base salary.[44] In the authors' experience, incentive percentages can be as low as 5 percent of base salary; they are rarely higher than 25 to 30 percent of base, except in trade associations, where they can be significantly higher. The board should explicitly budget for extra cash compensation if it has a reasonable expectation that the extra cash will be awarded.

As the basis for determining incentive eligibility, the board and the chief executive should, as we have noted, set annual performance goals. Using the balanced scorecard approach described in Chapter 2, the chief executive and the board can establish goals in the four key areas: mission, financial, internal operations, and innovation and learning for future excellence and viability.[45] The board and the chief executive then formally review performance in relation to these goals at the end of each year, and the board uses the results of the review to determine both incentive eligibility and eligibility for a base pay increase. The board may weight all the goals equally or weight some more heavily than others, depending on its priorities for the year.

[44] Quatt Associates, *2008 Not-for-Profit Compensation Survey;* PRM Consulting, 2008 *Management Compensation Report: Not-for-Profit Organizations,* p. 141.

[45] Robert S. Kaplan and David P. Norton, *Translating Strategy into Action: The Balanced Scorecard* (Boston: Harvard Business School Press, 1996).

In setting financial objectives, the board should be careful about directly awarding a percentage of money raised. As noted previously, setting a cap on revenue-based incentives can help ensure that the total paid does not create intermediate sanctions concerns, but incentives structured in this way are considered unethical by many nonprofits and may attract extra scrutiny from the IRS. The Association of Fundraising Professionals prohibits its members from receiving such compensation and states that, where compensation is percentage based, "charitable mission can become secondary to self-gain" and "there is incentive for self-dealing to prevail over donors' best interests."[46] Percentage-based rewards may also damage an organization's public image, especially at organizations that depend on donations from the general public for their funding. Such donations are made with the expectation that they will be used to accomplish the organization's mission. Those who make the donations may perceive a percentage-based fundraising award for the chief executive as the diversion of the organization's resources for personal gain, even if the award is capped and is part of a total compensation package that meets legal requirements regarding market reasonableness.

Not all chief executive incentive plans work. Without careful and continuing board involvement, an incentive plan can simply become an automatic addition to base salary. Once an incentive becomes an entitlement, it loses its ability to motivate the chief executive. In addition, a carelessly managed incentive plan can destroy morale among other nonprofit staff: If the chief executive receives an annual bonus whether or not the organization can point to identifiable achievements, staff may see the cash award as simply an extra, and undeserved, senior management perk. If a bonus or incentive plan is to be motivational and strategic, the board must be involved in setting objectives and must be rigorous in judging organizational and chief executive performance.

The same concerns apply to incentives for other senior executives. The chief executive needs to manage senior executive incentives (also a growing nonprofit trend) so that they are motivational and strategic, and based on a careful planning and governance process.

---

[46] Association of Fundraising Professionals, "Position Paper: Percentage-Based Compensation," www.afpnet.org/tier3_cd.cfm?folder_id=899&content_itemid=1227 (accessed February 11, 2005).

DETERMINING IF EXTRA CASH COMPENSATION MAKES SENSE FOR THE ORGANIZATION

The following questions should be asked by the compensation committee before taking the next step in creating an incentive program:

- Will adding an incentive better focus the organization and chief executive on key priorities?

- Is providing extra cash compensation customary in the organization's (nonprofit) marketplace?

- Is providing extra cash compensation consistent with the organization's culture?

- Can extra cash compensation help the organization manage compensation costs?

- Does the chief executive expect extra cash compensation as part of a competitive compensation package?

- Is the organization able to plan and set objectives effectively?

- Is the board willing to commit the time and effort needed to set objectives and to rate the chief executive annually in terms of those objectives?

- Will the board be able to act fairly, critically, and impartially in rating the chief executive?

SETTING UP AN INCENTIVE OR BONUS PROGRAM

1. Engage all stakeholders in the program.

   - For many nonprofit organizations, bonus or incentive programs are controversial. (We will refer to them as incentive programs, since the program should in principle motivate the participant to achieve a certain desired performance.) The compensation committee should engage stakeholders when considering an incentive program because their buy-in to both the existence and the design of the plan is essential.

2. Determine what purpose the incentive program will serve.

   - To improve organizational and/or chief executive performance?

   - To provide a more market-competitive salary?

   - To serve as a retention or deferred compensation vehicle for the executive?

   - To control base salary costs with an additional compensation opportunity (consistent with the market) if economic circumstances permit?

3. Determine how the incentive program will fit into the compensation and benefits plan and market competitiveness.

4. Determine the level of the incentive compensation relative to base salary and benefits.

  • The combination of base salary, incentive, and benefits needs to be consistent with the desired market position of the organization, and it cannot exceed comparable compensation practices if the organization is to avoid intermediate sanctions issues. (Incentive compensation cannot easily be added to base salary if base salary is already relatively high in comparison to the marketplace.)

  • Incentive compensation frequency and levels should be weighed against those of comparable organizations in the marketplace.

5. Determine the performance metrics appropriate for the incentive award.

  • How quantitative should the metrics be?

  • How can mission success or impact be measured? (We note that while mission measures are not always the easiest to measure, they are the most relevant measures of a nonprofit.)

  • What metrics might raise questions relative to the organization's mission or with stakeholders or the public? For instance, commissions tied to fundraising are not acceptable in many sectors.

6. Determine the process for setting performance goals and reviewing results.

  • What role will the board play?

  • What role will the chief executive play?

  • How will the board assess performance and assign an incentive amount?

7. Determine the plan design.

  • What is the level of incentive? A percentage of salary? A fixed dollar amount?

  • Should there be an incentive range or a fixed dollar range based on performance?

  • How is the incentive paid relative to the number of performance goals? Should some goals have higher weighting than others?

8. How will the incentive be funded? Will it be budgeted? Will it be contingent on the achievement of certain financial measures?

BEST PRACTICES FOR DESIGNING A PERFORMANCE MANAGEMENT PLAN

As discussed elsewhere (see page 87), we recommend a formal system for reviewing chief executive performance on an annual basis, with evaluation tied to the organization's annual governance process. Performance objectives for the coming year should be determined jointly by the chief executive and the board at the annual board meeting.

We recommend that performance objectives cover three areas: strategic objectives (we recommend creating objectives in each of the four categories of the Harvard Balanced Scorecard approach described in Chapter 2), performance in addressing unforeseen challenges, and general leadership. Goals should include concrete, realistic measures for success, as well as a system for rating success in meeting each objective. For example:

1 = failed to meet objectives

2 = partially successful in meeting objectives

3 = successful in meeting objectives

4 = exceeded objectives

The rating system should be linked to the incentive opportunity through a well-defined structure, so that the chief executive has a clear and accurate understanding of how his or her performance will be awarded prior to the evaluation period. We recommend an incentive opportunity with the following structure:

- Threshold. The threshold is the minimum incentive amount; if performance fails to meet a minimum level of success, no incentive will be awarded.

- Target. The target rewards performance that meets the criteria for full success.

- Maximum. The maximum is awarded if the chief executive's performance is outstanding, or far exceeds the measures established for full success. In awarding a maximum incentive amount, the board should check that the award does not cause total compensation to exceed reasonable market practice. The board should also be careful not to create the expectation on the part of the chief executive that he or she will receive the maximum regularly.

The overall rating should be based on the weighted average of ratings in the strategic, leadership, and performance against unforeseen challenges categories. Individual objectives may be given their own weighting, or the average of objectives in each category may be given a weighting (e.g., mission goals may be weighted as 30 percent of the overall rating).

Based on the ratings system above, an overall performance rating of between 2 and 3 would merit an award between the threshold and target amounts, and an overall rating of between 3 and 4 would merit an award between the target and maximum amounts.

The same ratings system can be applied to merit increases to base salary. For example, if the median increase in market base salary is 3 percent, full performance (i.e., a rating of 3) would warrant an increase of 3 percent. A lower performance rating would warrant a lower merit increase, and a higher rating would, within reason and in accordance with IRS rules, warrant a higher increase.

At its annual meeting, the board evaluates performance during the previous year based on the predetermined objectives. The appraisal process may take multiple forms: The board may have sole responsibility for a formal evaluation, or the chief executive may draft a self-evaluation, that is then reviewed by the board.

Example: Organization X is a major environmental advocacy organization. The organization has drafted a new strategic plan that seeks to pass a piece of major climate change legislation over the next several years, as well as implement a major new conservation program within the organization. Given the importance of these initiatives to the organization's future, it wants to link them to the incentive plan. It also wants to ensure that the incentive opportunity is large enough to provide the proper motivation.

The board examines the data it has gathered on the marketplace for the chief executive. The chief executive's compensation targets the median of the marketplace. The difference between the median of market total cash compensation and the chief executive's salary is equal to roughly 15 percent of her salary. Therefore, the board sets a target incentive opportunity equal to 15 percent of the chief executive's salary, with a threshold of 10 percent and a maximum of 20 percent.

The board then turns to the question of which objectives to include in the plan, using the categories set forth by the Harvard Balanced Scorecard approach. In the mission category, the board wants to focus on the legislation and conservation program. Because these are both multiyear initiatives, the board must decide what would constitute successful progress in the coming year. It confers with the chief executive, and they agree that success with regards to the legislative objective will be defined as securing the commitment through the personal lobbying of the chief executive of 10 co-sponsors in the House of Representatives (the chief executive confers with the head of government relations to ensure this is a realistic goal), and the airing of an ad campaign to build support for the bill. In terms of internal effectiveness, the chief executive and board also set goals for internal effectiveness (e.g., overhauling the IT system), finances, and innovation.

At the end of the year, the chief executive completes a self-evaluation, including ratings for each objective and an explanation for these ratings. The board reviews the evaluation, modifying the ratings as it sees fit, and gives an overall rating of 3.4. The chief executive has surpassed the measure of full success, and is entitled to an award above target. The board decides to give an award equal to 17 percent of salary, somewhat above target.

SIGN-ON AND RETENTION BONUSES

Sign-on bonuses are increasingly seen in the initial offer to chief executives of larger nonprofits. Retention bonuses are still relatively rare in nonprofit compensation, although not completely unknown.

Each type of bonus can be a useful part of a compensation package. A sign-on bonus is used for several purposes. (1) It can provide financial resources to the executive to cover transition costs; (2) it can allow for a competitive offer, while maintaining the initial base salary at a lower level; this may be desired for reasons including internal equity with other positions as well as a recognition that an executive's first year is usually a learning year; (3) it can provide an inducement for changing jobs. A retention bonus can encourage a long-term commitment to the organization, as well as providing a more competitive compensation package over the tenure of the executive. Such an arrangement may also be more palatable to stakeholders, since the organization gets in return for additional compensation assurance that the chief executive will stay for the entire retention period.

If a sign-on or retention bonus is part of the initial chief executive contract, it is protected from the intermediate sanctions regulations by the initial contract exception so long as the amount is fixed. However, no such bonus is protected from the scrutiny of press, public, or staff. Since both types of bonus can represent a substantial expense to the organization, both must be fully justified in terms of the organization's needs.

DEFERRED COMPENSATION

Deferred compensation is an increasingly common feature of nonprofit executive compensation plans, especially among larger nonprofits. Like all elements of compensation, it must be counted as part of total compensation for intermediate sanctions and private inurement purposes.

The term deferred compensation is used to cover two overlapping categories of future compensation.[47] In the broadest sense, deferred compensation refers to a portion of an executive's salary that is deferred for payment at some time in the future. In addition, the term deferred compensation is also used to refer to certain compensation arrangements that defer pay, tax-free, until retirement or some other vesting time.

A nonprofit might have one or more reasons for including deferred compensation, broadly defined, in its chief executive compensation package:

- Deferred compensation can support the organization's compensation strategy. The vesting period linked to a deferred compensation plan can, for example,

---

[47] Gregory L. Needles, Esq., and Boyd J. Brown, II, Esq., "Retirement Plans and Deferred Compensation for Tax Exempt Employees," Paper presented at Georgetown University Law Center Continuing Legal Education: Representing and Managing Tax-Exempt Organizations, April 25–26, 2002.

provide an incentive for the chief executive to stay in service to the organization; a chief executive's contract might specify a cash payment if the chief executive stays with the organization for three years. (In fact, one of the most common forms of deferred compensation, the 457(f) plan, requires that the executive remain with the organization until the end of the plan's vesting period, or the retention plan will be completely forfeit.) Future payments can also take the form of long-term incentives that are contingent on the achievement of certain goals.

- Deferred compensation can also help meet the chief executive's need for future income, especially in retirement. The special tax provisions described below are used principally, although not exclusively, for retirement-oriented deferred compensation. Retirement-oriented deferred compensation plans can be structured so they also support organizational goals, such as retention or the achievement of key performance objectives.

Deferred compensation arrangements are often complex and can have major tax and liability implications for both the organization and the chief executive. The chief executive and the board should retain legal counsel when drafting an agreement on deferred compensation. The brief description provided here of tax provisions and their possible advantages is no substitute for detailed advice from an experienced professional. For those organizations that may compete for talent with the for-profit sector, deferred compensation, even at the more modest and constrained level available for nonprofits, may help in partially leveling the playing field.

TAX-DEFERRED COMPENSATION

Tax-deferred compensation is most frequently used as a way of preparing for retirement. Before considering special plans for the chief executive, the compensation committee should ensure that it provides salary deferral opportunities to its entire staff through a 403(b) or a 401(k) plan. These plans allow both salary deferral and additional employer contributions for retirement. 501(c)(3) organizations and public employers are allowed to establish 403(b) plans; all employers other than state or local governments may establish 401(k) plans. Contribution limits under both types of plan are the same, but change regularly; organizations should look up annually the contribution limits, which can be found on the IRS Web site. The limit for elective employee deferrals is $16,500 in 2009. Total contributions are limited to $49,000 in employee and employer contributions or 100 percent of compensation, if compensation is less than $49,000. Employees over the age of 50 may also make additional "catch-up" deferrals. The maximum "catch-up" deferral for 2009 is $5,500. Under recently passed laws, organizations eligible to establish a 403(b) may also establish 401(k) plans. Organizations with both types of plan allow contributions to both.

Even when an organization has in place a savings plan for the organization as a whole, the chief executive may want additional opportunities for retirement savings because of the limits on the amounts that can be saved under a 403(b), 401(k), or 401(a) defined benefit plan. In addition to the absolute limits on the amount that can be contributed, the amount of salary that can be considered in calculating allowable contributions under qualified plans is capped at $245,000 in 2009. This cap is increased regularly. 401(k) and 403(b) plans are also subject to nondiscrimination rules that can limit the amount that employers can contribute on behalf of legally defined highly compensated employees such as the chief executive. The nondiscrimination tests for 403(b) plans are somewhat simpler than those for 401(k) plans, and churches and government entities are exempt from the nondiscrimination test requirement.

Special deferred compensation plans for retirement are common among larger and more complex nonprofits. In one 2008 national nonprofit survey, 52 percent of chief executives surveyed had a deferred compensation or supplemental retirement plan in addition to standard defined benefit or defined contribution plans.[48] Among the participants in Quatt Associates' 2008 survey of major trade associations in the Washington, D.C., area, 48 percent provided deferred compensation to the chief executive. Among participants in Quatt Associates' 2008 survey of major foundations, advocacy organizations, and media and cultural organizations, 31 percent provided deferred compensation to their chief executive.[49] Since these surveys include only larger organizations, the percentage of all U.S. nonprofits with such arrangements is probably somewhat lower.

The two principal nonqualified vehicles for tax-deferred compensation are designated by their Internal Revenue Code sections: 457(b) and 457(f). They are called "non-qualified" because they are not officially recognized as retirement plans by the IRS.

457(B) PLANS

Nonprofit employees may defer income tax-free by participating in a 457(b) plan as well as a 401(k) or 403(b). 457(b) plans are limited to senior staff members (as a rule of thumb, no more than 10 percent of total staff) and hence are a variety of "top hat" plan (a plan only for top positions — typically executives). The contribution limit for 457(b) plans is the same as that for 401(k) and 403(b) plans: $16,500 for 2009, but changing regularly. Therefore, by creating a 457(b) plan, a nonprofit organization with an existing 401(k) or 403(b) plan can double the amount of compensation its senior employees can defer free of taxes.

Unlike 401(k) and 403(b) plans, which are the property of participating employees, a 457(b) plan is legally the property of the employer and is subject to creditors' claims until such time as it actually becomes available to the participant or

---

[48] PRM Consulting, *2008 Management Compensation Report; Not-for-Profit Organizations,* p. 146.

[49] Quatt Associates, *2008 Trade Association CEO Compensation and Benefits Survey; 2008 Not-for-Profit Survey.*

beneficiary. Funds from a 457(b) plan cannot be distributed until separation from employment, or in the event of serious unforeseeable emergency.

A 457(b) plan can either allow the organization to increase compensation to senior executives in a way that defers taxes, or allow senior executives to defer more of their current salaries. In order to provide this latter option, therefore, organizations may wish to establish 457(b) plans even when they do not intend to use them to provide additional compensation to senior staff. Alternatively, payments to a 457(b) can be tied to the achievement of annual or long-term goals, and thus serve as a retention and/or incentive vehicle as well as means of saving for retirement.

457(F) PLANS

Nonprofits may also establish 457(f) plans. These plans have no limit on contributions, and taxes are deferred as long as the employee faces a legally defined substantial risk of forfeiture. The substantial risk of forfeiture generally takes the form of a vesting schedule, such as a promise to continue employment for a certain number of years. Such a schedule can, and often does, serve as the vehicle for a retention incentive or reward for performance; receipt of the 457(f) funds is contingent on fulfilling the requirement. The IRS takes the substantial risk of forfeiture requirement very seriously — a chief executive who leaves early does in fact forfeit the 457(f).

Once the substantial risk of forfeiture ends — for example, when the employee has completed the contract term — the full amount of the amount deferred is taxable. This can create substantial tax liabilities for a chief executive in the year of vesting.

Some organizations explicitly fund their 457(f) plans, while others simply promise to pay at some point in the future. Like 457(b) plans, 457(f) plans legally belong to the organization and are subject to the claims of creditors.

457(f) plans are much more complicated than 457(b) or other saving and retirement vehicles. Both the organization's board and the chief executive should understand the conditions of the 457(f) plan, the risk of forfeiture, and the tax consequences of vesting. Drafting and review of the plan by an experienced lawyer and accountant is essential.

SPLIT DOLLAR LIFE INSURANCE PLANS

Some nonprofits in the past have used a so-called split dollar life insurance plan as a nonqualified deferred compensation vehicle. Under a split dollar plan, the nonprofit pays either all or the majority of the chief executive's personal life insurance policy premiums. Ownership of the life insurance policy is split between the chief executive and the organization. The organization pays the premiums and is entitled to receive the value of the premiums upon the death of the employee. The employee or the beneficiaries receive the earnings on the premiums advanced.

The IRS has been skeptical about split dollar life insurance plans. Under regulations issued on September 17, 2003, split dollar life insurance plans are no longer a suitable instrument for deferring taxes. While in some cases an organization might still be interested in a split dollar plan as a life insurance vehicle, it should seek experienced legal advice before adopting such a plan.

DEFERRED COMPENSATION IN SUMMARY

Deferred compensation can be an attractive part of a compensation package, both for an organization and for its chief executive. It can support retention and encourage achievement of performance goals while helping a chief executive save for retirement. Providing further opportunities for tax-deferred compensation through increased funding of a 457(b) or through a 457(f) can make sense in some circumstances, especially for chief executives at the higher end of the market. Sophisticated and experienced legal and accounting advice is essential in considering such options.

As noted previously, all deferred compensation must be taken into account in determining total compensation for purposes of the intermediate sanctions regulations. Deferred compensation will also be reported twice on the organization's IRS Form 990: once in the year earned, and then again when it vests. (Although the new 990 will allow organizations to identify previous accrued compensation.) For some organizations, this may generate undesirable impressions in the public eye.

Q I think our chief executive receives too many benefits. How can I determine the appropriate level?

A From a legal perspective, the key issue is the amount of total compensation, which means base pay plus any incentives and benefits. That amount should be compared to the market, as explained in Chapter 5. Assuming the total amount of pay is reasonable when compared with the market, your next step would be to review standard survey data, which will typically include information on the prevalence of particular benefits. A review of such data can help you decide if your organization's practices are out of line with the market. Ultimately, however, the decision on what is appropriate will require weighing the cost of the benefits and other payments that your organization makes to the chief executive against the chief executive's value to the organization.

OTHER BENEFITS AND PERQUISITES

Nonprofit organizations offer a range of benefits and perquisites to their chief executives. Quatt's 2008 survey of pay practices at large nonprofits found that the middle 50 percent (from the 25th percentile to 75th percentile) of benefits as a percentage of salary was 9 percent to 26 percent.[50] Each organization's compensation committee must make its own decision as to what mix of benefits and perquisites

---

[50] Quatt Associates, 2008 *Not-for-Profit Compensation Survey.*

makes sense by looking at market practice, the organization's culture and history, and the types of activities in which the chief executive is expected to engage.

Nearly all organizations provide the standard health insurance benefits, and many also provide disability and a modest amount of life insurance. Smaller organizations can often find cost-effective approaches to providing insurance through local nonprofit associations that have group plans.

A number of other benefit and perquisite possibilities also exist (please see the following page for a list of options). The authors recommend that compensation committees avoid including the less common options in their chief executive compensation packages unless the inclusion of one or more will result in a demonstrable benefit to the organization.

Q Should we provide a small mortgage to our chief executive?

A Housing assistance is a relatively uncommon, although not unknown, benefit among nonprofits. Many colleges and universities, for example, provide housing to their chief executives, with the expectation that the residence will be used frequently to entertain potential donors.

Some nonprofits also provide low-interest or no-interest loans to their chief executives. Such loans do not constitute an excess benefit transaction per se, since the chief executive must repay the loan. The interest subsidy (i.e., the amount by which the interest rate falls below fair market value), however, is private compensation and must be taken into account in determining the reasonableness of compensation for legal purposes. The interest subsidy may also be a taxable benefit to the chief executive. Some states (for example, the District of Columbia) prohibit loans to nonprofit officers and directors. The size and creditworthiness of the borrower should also be taken into account. A loan that represents a large portion of the organization's assets, for example, may violate the private inurement doctrine. From a public perception standpoint, any loan should be justifiable in terms of its benefit to the organization.

Benefits, including the market value of housing and transportation and other similar benefits, must generally be included in the intermediate sanctions calculation (there is an exception if use of employee-provided housing is required).[51] Perquisites, such as first-class or charter travel, travel for companions, tax indemnification and gross-up payments, a discretionary spending account, a housing allowance, residence for personal use or other personal services, can be a lightning rod for public scrutiny, and compensation committees should be very careful before approving anything that may seem out of the ordinary, excessive, or inappropriate to the culture and history of the organization. Boards should also check with legal counsel to understand which benefits might be taxable; chief executives may prefer simply receiving direct compensation rather than a benefit for which they would be required to pay taxes.

---

[51] Housing is a non-taxable benefit for employees of an academic institution or other 501(c)(3) when it meets a three-part test: (1) the employee is required to accept the housing as a condition of employment (2) the housing is located on the institution's business premises and (3) the housing is furnished for the convenience of the institution. IRC 119 (a)

LIST OF BENEFITS OPTIONS FOR CHIEF EXECUTIVES

Relatively common benefits:

- Retirement benefits, either in the form of defined contribution plans, such as a 401(k) or 403(b) plan, or (now less common) a defined benefit pension plan

- Benefits that apply to all employees in the organization, including life insurance, health coverage, short-term and long-term disability, etc.

- Supplemental life, health, and disability insurance (life insurance may be taxable) — particularly when the all-employee plan has a cap that may prevent the chief executive or other executives from receiving the full benefit

- Memberships in professional organizations and subscriptions to professional journals

- Annual physical exams

- Car or transportation allowance (taxable if not for business purposes)

- Parking privileges

- Severance provisions in the chief executive contract (see page 115)

Specialized situation benefits:

- Housing allowance (including low-interest or no-interest mortgage loans), maintenance, and utilities; this benefit is most common among nonprofits such as colleges and universities whose chief executives are expected to entertain donors frequently, and organizations in areas with high costs of living; these benefits may be taxable unless they meet special IRS exceptions, e.g., for colleges and universities (see page 101, footnote 51)

- Sabbaticals: Most common in educational and religious organizations

- Entertainment budget: Most common among larger nonprofits whose chief executives are expected to do extensive networking and entertaining on the organization's behalf

- Tuition assistance: Most common in the college and university environment, but can be provided by other types of nonprofits (likely to be taxable)

Less common or emerging benefits:

- Social club or country club memberships (common among trade associations but not among charities)

- Financial counseling

- First-class air travel

- Spouse travel (likely to be taxable, and a favorite target of IRS scrutiny)

- Excess liability insurance

- Higher (or no) cap on long-term disability (this is very rare)

- Long-term care insurance

THE FINAL COMPENSATION PACKAGE

The compensation committee puts together the initial version of the organization's chief executive compensation package, but the final package will be based on negotiations between the committee or full board and the candidate for the position. A wise board will enter those negotiations armed not only with knowledge of what the market allows, but also with a sense of the compensation elements it will be comfortable with in negotiation and the limits on negotiation of those elements. In developing the final compensation package, some questions to consider include

- How does the overall compensation and benefits package compare to the marketplace? Is it defensible to both the IRS and stakeholders?

- Does the compensation package reflect a strategic compensation philosophy? Do the individual elements of the package make sense? For instance, what sort of sign-on bonus or retention bonus is advantageous for the organization? How will stakeholders, including the public and the employees of the organization, feel about the compensation plan (don't forget, it will be publicly disclosed through the 990)?

- For validation purposes, does the board need an outside opinion on the reasonableness of the compensation package?

- Beyond base salary, is the board open in principle to incentive compensation, and does it feel capable of administering an incentive system? Is the board ready and willing to develop an incentive compensation plan and to incorporate the management of the incentive compensation plan into its governance process?

- Does the organization need a deferred compensation arrangement such as described in this book, and does the board want to bear the legal and accounting costs of establishing such a system, not to mention the possible costs in terms of public scrutiny?

- What is the right benefits and perquisites package for the organization? Is the package market competitive? Is the package consistent with the organization's compensation philosophy and its traditions? How far beyond tradition might the organization be willing to go in establishing a new or enhanced benefits plan and will the stakeholders support it?

Asking and answering these questions beforehand will make for a clearer and more open negotiating process with the new chief executive and a higher level of comfort with the final package.

The full board should carefully review and approve the final compensation package. If the compensation package under consideration is for a sitting chief executive (i.e., not subject to the initial contract exception), careful review of every aspect of the compensation package, as well as the total compensation amount is essential. It guards against the board approving a package that risks intermediate sanctions scrutiny, and, if conducted properly, protects board members from personal liability by establishing the rebuttable presumption of reasonableness. A careful review also forces the board to anticipate any public scrutiny of the compensation package, and whether and how the package can be justified in terms of the financial constraints of the budget.

SUMMARY: ACTION STEPS FOR THE BOARD

- Identify the elements to be included in the compensation package, keeping in mind the total value of all elements; the value of total compensation is the standard for the legal tests described in Chapter 6.

- Identify the parameters beyond which the board cannot will not go in terms of both total compensation and individual elements of the package.

- Set base salary in light of the market data obtained from following the steps outlined in Chapter 5.

  o If the board is in the process of negotiating to hire or retain a chief executive, determine a range within which the board is willing to negotiate.

- If the board decides to include incentive compensation in the compensation plan, it should compare the total cash compensation opportunity it wishes to provide to the level of total cash it wishes to target in the marketplace, setting salary by subtracting the extra cash opportunity from marketplace total cash compensation.

- Decide whether base salary will be constant for the duration of the contract, or if it will be adjusted annually based on performance and movement in the salary market.

  o If the board decides to adjust salary annually, it must also decide the process for making the adjustment, and the data upon which it will base the adjustment.

- Decide the process for assessing annual performance and awarding bonuses or incentives, if included in the compensation plan.

  o We recommend that a formal performance evaluation process be added to the board's annual governance process; specific performance objectives should be set prior to the evaluation period, with clear instructions on how rewards connect with performance.

- Understand the reasons for including incentive compensation.

  o If it decides to include an incentive compensation plan, the board should tie awards to performance.

  o The board should understand that incentive plans that directly award the chief executive a percentage of fundraising are viewed as unethical by many and may attract scrutiny from the IRS.

- Understand the reasons for offering a sign-on or retention bonus, taking into account the fact that such bonuses remain rare at nonprofits, and that they must be fully justified so as not to attract unwanted scrutiny.

- Understand the reasons for including deferred compensation in the total compensation package, and be aware of the available options.

- Understand the other benefits and perquisites available.

  o Be careful about including less common benefits; we recommend that such benefits only be included if they provide a demonstrable return benefit to the organization.

  o Be careful about including benefits that may appear excessive by their nature or do not fit the organizational culture; these may attract public scrutiny.

- Be aware that the value of most benefits must be reported on the organization's 990.

- Have counsel review the compensation, and determine which benefits are taxable.

- Once the compensation committee is comfortable with the package, ensure that it is reviewed and approved by the full board.

CHAPTER 9
TERM NEGOTIATIONS AND THE FINAL CONTRACT

The final step in the chief executive compensation process is to establish the terms of the chief executive's employment, including the final compensation package, and then formalize the relationship in writing. A formal and detailed written contract is desirable, but smaller nonprofits not wanting to go to the legal expense of drafting a detailed agreement should still put together a written memorandum of agreement that lays out salary, benefits, and the period of employment.

Q **What are the advantages/disadvantages of chief executive employment contracts? How common is the practice? What should be included? What should be the duration?**

A Organizations should draft a formal employment contract in all but the simplest employment relationships. A formal contract provides security to both the executive and to the board, and makes absolutely clear the details of the compensation arrangement and the mutual expectations of the two parties. The employment contract also offers some added security to both the executive and the organization by demonstrating the organization's commitment to the executive. In our experience, a formal contract is increasingly common.

The most important elements of a chief executive contract are listed in Chapter 8. A typical contract duration is three to five years; three years is most common in our experience.

NEGOTIATING EMPLOYMENT TERMS

Whether developing a contract renewal for an existing chief executive or negotiating a contract for a new chief executive, the terms of employment should be based on a current job description and a compensation package that is typically developed by a board committee, such as a compensation committee, executive committee, or a specially constituted negotiating committee. Whatever the arrangement, the contract terms should be approved by the full board. Both the board negotiators and the candidate need to prepare for these negotiations in specific ways. The following lists will be helpful, especially in the case of a new candidate for the position.

FIND THE RIGHT FIT

THE CANDIDATE	THE BOARD
• The candidate should understand the needs of the organization, including its mission, objectives, and culture, and determine his or her ability to meet those needs. • The candidate should understand what is expected in terms of position responsibilities and performance objectives. • The candidate should determine if the organization is the best fit with his or her interests, skills, and preferred career path.	• The board should identify the needs of the organization based on its review of organizational strategy and objectives, and its understanding of the organizational history and culture. • The board should identify the primary leadership expectations for the chief executive, and the qualifications and experience that will make the chief executive successful in carrying out the organization's mission, effectively engaging with key stakeholders, and exemplifying the desired culture of the organization. It should recruit and prescreen candidates based on those needs. • The board should also keep in mind that challenges and leadership needs change. What made a successful chief executive in the past may be different now. • The board should explain its expectations for the chief executive in terms of position responsibilities and performance objectives.

UNDERSTAND THE ROLE OF COMPENSATION
IN THE ORGANIZATION

THE CANDIDATE	THE BOARD
• The candidate should ask the board its view of compensation and the role compensation plays in the organization. • The candidate should understand the constraints that the organization's financial status, history, and culture put on compensation level and structure. • The candidate should understand, if possible, the organization's current compensation practices, including base salary levels, compensation increase practices, and incentive practice (if any), and use 990 data to learn how the previous chief executive and other high-level employees were paid. • The candidate should recognize that the compensation of his or her predecessor may be higher than the compensation that might be offered to the new candidate (the past incumbent may have, for example, been very long serving, or had special skills and experience). • The candidate should be aware that the heightened scrutiny of nonprofit chief executive compensation may place constraints on compensation that were not present with the previous chief executive, that the entire compensation process will be more transparent than in the past, and that there may be a greater likelihood of resistance from some stakeholders to a compensation proposal. • The candidate must recognize that the entire compensation package will be disclosed on the 990, probably in greater detail than before. He or she must consider the implications of that disclosure in terms of public and stakeholder reaction, and the impact that will have on the organization, and on the candidate's reputation.	• The board should define the role of compensation in the organization (its compensation philosophy) and understand what constraints the organization's financial status, history, and culture put on compensation level and structure. • The board should consider public and stakeholder scrutiny of its chief executive pay practices.

UNDERSTAND THE MARKETPLACE

THE CANDIDATE	THE BOARD
• The candidate needs to understand the marketplace — what organizations similar in size, location, and mission typically pay, and how the pay is structured in terms of base pay, bonuses and incentives, and typical benefits and perquisites. • The candidate should also understand that the marketplace may limit compensation as compared to the candidate's previous employment.	• The board needs to understand the marketplace — what organizations similar in size, location, and mission typically pay, and how the pay is structured. Understanding the marketplace will also enable the board to determine how the intermediate sanctions regulations may limit compensation. • The board needs to be prepared to define limits to the compensation offer above which it may not wish to go or may not be able to go.

UNDERSTAND OPTIONS FOR COMPENSATION

THE CANDIDATE	THE BOARD
• The candidate should ask the board for its initial concept of how the compensation plan will work, including base salary increase plan, incentive compensation, and benefits.	• Based on the organization's financial status, needs, and culture, and the marketplace, the board should make an initial determination of how compensation will be structured, how the chief executive's performance will be measured, and what linkage there will be between pay and performance. • The board should prepare a draft compensation plan, including a base salary range and expected benefits within reasonable marketplace practices. It may also include performance-based compensation and a plan for annual salary increases.

UNDERSTAND COMPENSATION REQUIREMENTS

THE CANDIDATE	THE BOARD
• The candidate should understand his or her compensation and benefits needs, ranking them in order of importance. • If the candidate is relinquishing a retirement benefit or long-term compensation opportunity, the candidate should understand what the impact is on his or her retirement plans. For instance, the candidate might want to negotiate for a deferred compensation plan to provide retirement savings as part of the compensation plan. The candidate needs to understand the long-term financial implications of the compensation options in relation to his or her financial needs and retirement planning. The candidate may wish to engage a financial planner. If so, familiarity with nonprofit pay practices and legal requirements is essential.	• The board should discuss the candidate's compensation requirements with the candidate. This is often accomplished at first through a third party such as a search consultant or the organization's human resources department.

CONTRACT

THE CANDIDATE	THE BOARD
• The candidate needs to determine whether a contract is desirable from his or her perspective. A formal contract can clarify the expectations of both parties. The protection of a contract can be especially useful for the chief executive, who will clearly understand how the salary and incentive (if any) will be managed, how performance will be assessed, and what the details of the severance agreement would be.	• The board needs to determine whether a contract is desirable. A formal contract can clarify the expectations of both parties, and is especially helpful in laying out the process for salary adjustments, performance measurement, incentive compensation guidelines, and severance practice. continued on next page

THE CANDIDATE	THE BOARD
• If a contract is required by the organization, the candidate needs to understand the terms of the contract. • Legal assistance for the candidate can be helpful in negotiating the contract.	• Compensation structure and level should be reflected in the contract. The contract should include the starting salary; the process for adjusting salary, e.g., at board discretion or based on a preselected index; incentive or bonus levels and process; benefits — both standard and executive — and severance provisions, including termination policy, required notice, severance payment, benefits continuance, and others. • Drafting the contract requires the assistance of an attorney.

GOOD WILL AND FLEXIBILITY

THE CANDIDATE	THE BOARD
• The candidate needs to determine how flexible to be in the salary negotiation. What is the minimum acceptable salary? What benefits are essential? How can salary and benefits or perquisites be traded off? • Salary negotiations should be conducted in good faith, positively and professionally. This is the beginning of what is hoped to be a long and productive relationship. Too contentious or confrontational a contract negotiation can get the relationship off on the wrong footing.	• The board needs to determine how flexible it can be in the salary negotiation. What range of salary is it open to? Which options are acceptable, and which are unacceptable? • Salary negotiations should be conducted in good faith, positively and professionally. This is the beginning of what is hoped to be a long and productive relationship. Too contentious or confrontational a contract negotiation can get the relationship off on the wrong footing.

WRITING THE EMPLOYMENT CONTRACT

Many nonprofit organizations never take the final step of formalizing the relationship with the chief executive in a written contract. A 2008 national survey of nonprofit organizations reports that 45 percent of participants (mostly larger nonprofits) had formal employment agreements with their chief executives,[52] However, the authors encourage organizations to draft a formal employment contract or memorandum of agreement, even in the simplest employment relationships. Having a formal written agreement is advantageous for a number of reasons:

1. It makes the details of the compensation arrangement clear; together with the compensation committee's documentation of its decision-making process, it thus provides support for the reasonableness of the chief executive's compensation.

2. It provides a job description that outlines what the chief executive is expected to do, how and how often performance will be evaluated, and how compensation is tied to job performance.

3. It can articulate governance practices related to chief executive compensation and performance management. This can include how compensation decisions will be made annually with respect to base salary increases and incentive compensation, and how chief executive performance goals will be established annually and assessed at the end of the year.

4. It provides assurance that the terms that were discussed in negotiations will be honored.

5. It demonstrates the organization's commitment to the chief executive.

In short, a formal contract provides security to both the chief executive and to the organization and its board. By laying out the job description and compensation terms in writing, it ensures that mutual expectations are clear from the outset of the relationship. Even in the absence of a formal and detailed contract, we urge, as noted above, that the organization create a written summary of the terms of employment.

The contract will typically be drafted by the organization's in-house attorneys, if it has them, or by outside counsel. The chief executive candidate may also be represented by counsel in the drafting of the contract, but this is not always the case.

A typical contract includes the essential terms of employment. The following box lists the elements that might be included; the contract for a specific nonprofit will include only those that form part of its particular chief executive compensation package.

See Appendix V on page 145 for a sample chief executive contract that includes most of the items listed in the box that follows.

---

[52] PRM Consulting, *2008 Management Compensation Report: Not-for-Profit Organizations.*

ELEMENTS TO INCLUDE IN A CHIEF EXECUTIVE EMPLOYMENT CONTRACT

- The **term of the contract** and provision for contract renewal: A term of three years is most common in our experience, but longer or shorter terms are possible. Five year contracts also occur with some frequency, especially among chief executives renewing their contracts. Contracts will often have an option to renew the contract on mutual agreement of the parties.

- **A job description:** This may be attached as an appendix.

- The **starting salary**

- **Salary adjustment terms:** A schedule for future salary levels over the life of the contract, or language explaining how the salary will be adjusted going forward; in the latter case, salary may either be increased based on increases in the marketplace, or increased at the discretion of the board based on performance and the market (readers will know by now that we recommend the final option — based on performance and the market)

- **Incentive plans and performance bonuses:** What the level or range of incentive will be. How the incentive or bonus will work and how the incentive or bonus amount will be determined if there is a range. (We note that it is important to establish a level or range for incentive compensation. We have encountered situations where the board felt it had given a significant incentive to indicate strong performance and the chief executive was disappointed in the amount. A pre-established incentive range avoids this kind of misunderstanding.)

- **Evaluation:** How often, how, and by whom the chief executive's performance will be assessed

- **Retention bonus:** The amount to be paid if the chief executive stays for a certain term, either as a single amount paid at the end of the contract or as a stepped retention bonus with an amount paid out at stages over the life of the contract

- **Retirement/savings plan benefits**

- **Deferred compensation:** This may be covered in the retirement plan.

- **Benefits and perquisites:** Health and other insurance coverage, as well as other benefits provided as part of the overall employment agreement

- **Reimbursement of expenses:** Types of expenses that will be reimbursed, and the terms of reimbursement

- **Noncompetition agreement:** Such an agreement prohibits the executive from engaging in private consulting work that may compete with the work of the organization. Upon the executive's departure, this agreement may also set restrictions on future business dealings as well as restrictions on whom the executive may hire away from the organization. Organizations need to be careful that such a clause, if included, is not so restrictive or punitive that it discourages applicants.

- **Confidentiality clause:** Ensures that any nonpublic information that is confidential or privileged to the organization will not be made publicly available

- **Conflict-of-interest provision:** Describes potential conflicts of interest and indicates ways of preventing such conflicts

- **Termination clauses:** A provision stipulating with-cause termination releases the chief executive without severance benefits. With-cause termination is often a result of legal wrongdoing. Contracts that stipulate without-cause termination allow organizations to release the executive for poor performance or other related reasons, but the organization is typically obligated to pay severance benefits with termination.

- **Severance provisions:** This may be part of the contract or may be a separate document. See the Severance discussion below.

- **Arbitration:** How conflicts over the contract will be resolved

- **Governing law:** Identifies the state or jurisdiction under whose law the contract will be interpreted

SEVERANCE

Letting a chief executive go is one of the most difficult challenges for any board. In the absence of a contractual provision or other stated policy, the board is under no obligation to provide severance benefits to the chief executive. If there is a severance policy, it is typically set out as part of the chief executive's contract. A severance policy has several purposes:

- It may be necessary, since many chief executive candidates want severance provisions spelled out before accepting a position.

- It can serve as a retention vehicle for the chief executive, since voluntary departure generally does not trigger severance.

- It is common market practice and therefore contributes to the competitiveness of the compensation package.

- It reduces risk for both the chief executive and the board.

- It assures the candidate that, if the needs of the organization change, the candidate will have time to look for other work. This helps compensate candidates for the risk they take in leaving their current positions. Since it takes longer usually for a chief executive to find a comparable new position, chief executive severance is usually longer than that for other employees.

- It assures the board that if the needs of the organization change or the chief executive falls short of expectations, it can look for a new chief executive without causing undue harm to the current incumbent.

- It can help minimize any bad feeling between the former chief executive and the organization, as well as protect the organization from unfavorable publicity or legal action over claims by either party. The severance agreement will typically include a legal waiver and a promise of confidentiality.

Severance pay is almost universal in our experience among larger nonprofit organizations, and a 2009 study by Lee Hecht Harrison found that 54 percent of nonprofits offered severance benefits.[53] A typical severance package includes the following provisions:

- Notice provision: Allows the board to terminate the chief executive at its discretion so long as it gives appropriate notice (30 days' notice is common)

- Termination for cause: Allows the board to terminate the chief executive for cause without any notice. For cause generally means in the event of fraud or dishonesty, conviction of a felony or other major criminal or ethical offense, or failure to perform the duties of the position. No severance is paid in such cases.

- Severance payment: In the authors' experience and based on survey data, median market practice is to provide severance of one year's salary. Typically a severance plan is structured either as a flat amount (e.g., six months' or a year's pay) or an amount based on length of service with a minimum amount (e.g., six months plus one month for every year served). If based on length of service, there is often a cap on total severance: one year's pay is the most common amount, but a 24 months' cap also appears in some contracts. We would not recommend going above a 24 month cap.

- Outplacement services

- Continuation of benefits for a certain period of time

- House repurchase or relocation assistance

- Nondisclosure (i.e., the chief executive agrees not to divulge any confidential information regarding the organization)

- Legal waiver of any claims

- No disparagement of the organization

- Future cooperation

No board wants to contemplate the possibility of its chief executive failing to meet expectations, or of its relationship with the chief executive becoming negative or unproductive. However, such things do happen, and a written contract and severance policy can be immensely helpful if and when they do. By putting in writing all of the terms for the chief executive's employment and dismissal, the board ensures that it will be able to manage difficult situations if they do occur, and protects the investment of time and resources that it has made in the complex process of developing its chief executive compensation package.

---

[53] Lee Hecht Harrison, *Severance and Separation Practices: Benchmark Study 2008–2009.*

SUMMARY: ACTION STEPS FOR THE BOARD

- Ensure that the designated body of the board has drawn up a current position description and a compensation package it will offer the chief executive/candidate.

- Ensure that board negotiators and the chief executive/candidate understand and are prepared to engage in the negotiating process.

- Ensure that the board and chief executive/candidate understand the value of a written employment contract.

  o We recommend a formal employment contract, in lieu of which a formal memorandum or summary of the terms of employment should be created.

- Understand the items and provisions, which the contract should cover.

  o Understand the advantages of including a severance policy, and the typical severance provisions.

- If the board decides to institute a formal contract, it should be drafted by in-house or external counsel.

- Whatever the form of agreement, final terms and documents should be reviewed and approved by the full board.

CONCLUSION

The chief executive compensation package is an important component of a board's responsibility to the nonprofit it governs, and putting the package together is a complex activity. For this very reason, however, it provides the board with valuable opportunities.

Chief executive compensation is tied to who the chief executive is professionally (his or her credentials, accomplishments, life experiences, leadership qualities, and personal capabilities), as well as to what the chief executive is expected to do for the organization. Setting the chief executive's compensation thus gives the board an opportunity to review the organization's mission, priorities, and goals in order to define the attributes that it seeks in a chief executive and the objectives that it wants the chief executive to accomplish. It also gives the board an opportunity to review the marketplace in order to determine what chief executives at similar organizations do and how they are compensated. By taking advantage of these opportunities and documenting its work, the board ensures that its chief executive compensation decisions will be in compliance with the legal requirements related to private inurement and intermediate sanctions.

Chief executive compensation, along with other financial management practices at nonprofits, has become the subject of intense public scrutiny. The compensation package cannot be hidden; it is reported on the organization's tax returns, which are available in the public domain. Setting the chief executive's compensation thus gives the board an opportunity to think about the organization's public image and the ways in which the chief executive compensation package can affect it, either positively or negatively. It also gives the board an opportunity to review the compensation structure across the organization. By taking advantage of these opportunities and maintaining an appropriate degree of transparency, the board assures the organization's staff that the chief executive's compensation is part of a coherent compensation structure for all employees, and assures the organization's donors and volunteers that the organization's finances are being handled wisely and well.

In every nonprofit organization, whatever its mission, history, or size, chief executive compensation is an important oversight responsibility for the board. Small nonprofits are subject to the same legal standards as medium-sized and large ones, including intermediate sanctions. To ensure compliance while making the development of the chief executive compensation package as productive a process as possible, all boards need to remember the following basic guidelines:

1. Establish a clear process and institutional structure for setting chief executive compensation, defining the steps in the process, and who will be responsible for each.

2. Review the organization's mission, priorities, and goals and align the chief executive's role and compensation with them.

3. Develop a job title and a clear job description, and profile the characteristics and skills that a candidate must have to be successful.

4. Develop a compensation philosophy that embodies the organization's overall culture, values, critical goals, and mission. The compensation philosophy should cover the whole organization, and compensation for the chief executive should not be out of line with the principles upon which compensation for staff is based.

5. Gather information about the marketplace of comparable organizations in order to know what levels and types of compensation are appropriate. Regardless of the organization's size, the chief executive compensation plan cannot exceed the market. The IRS intermediate sanctions regulations allow organizations with $1 million or less in gross annual revenue to use compensation data from three comparable organizations in the same or similar communities for similar services; larger organizations must draw data from the larger marketplace. To reduce the burden of finding and using market information, look to local or regional sources such as associations for information that is available for free or at low cost, and use GuideStar for free information on compensation practices.

6. Obtain professional advice to ensure that the chief executive compensation package will meet the "front page test" as well as legal standards. Recruit a board member or other stakeholder who is familiar with compensation practices and can provide assistance. Pro bono or low-cost assistance from attorneys and compensation consultants is often available through local nonprofit associations, as well as through professional organizations such as Lawyers for the Arts.

7. Keep the compensation plan as simple as possible, and the process of developing it transparent.

8. Ensure that all board members are fully aware of all the elements of the compensation package as well as the total amount, and have reviewed the information reported on the annual IRS Form 990. Ensure that the final compensation package is approved by all board members.

9. Be completely open and forthcoming with the public, the press, and any other interested parties. The board should have nothing to hide about its compensation practices.

Following these guidelines will not always protect board members from having to answer questions about chief executive compensation, but it will give the board members the support they need to defend their answers; the compensation package is part of the board's responsibility and one of the elements for which the board is accountable to the organization's stakeholders and the general public. However, a board that follows these guidelines and the process outlined in this book will have a far easier time responding to any questions that are raised, whether by the IRS, the press, or the organization's donors and other stakeholders. Additionally, and perhaps more significantly, the members of the board — and the chief executive — will know that they have done their best to fulfill their responsibility to the organization they serve.

APPENDIX I
THE NEW IRS FORM 990

The new 990 form requires nonprofit organizations to report more detailed compensation information than before, for a greater number of employees. Organizations must now report compensation of all current officers, directors, trustees, and "key employees" (defined as those employees making over $150,000, with substantial influence over the organization, and among the 20 highest paid employees). In addition, organizations must report compensation of the five highest compensated employees making over $100,000 who are not officers, directors, trustees, or key employees. We strongly recommend that organizations consult with experienced counsel to ensure that all necessary staff members are included.

For every eligible employee, the organization must report name and title, average hours per week, position, taxable compensation, and estimated amount of other compensation, including deferred compensation, retirement contributions, and health benefits.

Employees who earned more than $150,000 will also be reported on Schedule J, where organizations must break out compensation by category, including base compensation, bonus and incentive compensation, deferred compensation, and nontaxable benefits. This is a significant change from the old 990, which reported only total cash compensation, benefits and deferred compensation (as one sum), and payments to expense accounts. Now organizations will have access to information about not only the pay levels of chief executives at comparable organizations, but also the ways in which compensation is structured, including typical bonus levels (assuming they are paid over $150,000 annually).

- Nonprofit organizations must report compensation of
    - o All officers
    - o All directors
    - o All trustees
    - o All key employees
        - * A key employee is an employee who satisfies the following three requirements:
        - * Is making over $150,000 in taxable compensation

* Has substantial influence over the organization (equivalent to that of officers, directors, or trustees, or in control of a division or functions representing at least 10 percent of the organization)

* Is among the organization's 20 highest paid employees

o The five highest compensated employees (other than officers, directors, trustees, and key employees) who received taxable compensation of more than $100,000

- For all employees listed above, the organization must report

    o Name and title

    o Average hours worked per week

    o Position

    o Taxable compensation

    o Estimated amount of other compensation (includes deferred compensation, retirement plan contributions, and health benefits) (we note that this requires estimating the value of pension fund contributions, a category frequently omitted in the past; estimating pension fund value can be challenging)

- Employees making $150,000 or more must also be reported in Schedule J, which requires compensation to be divided among the following categories:

    o Base compensation

    o Bonus and incentive compensation

    o Other taxable compensation

    o Deferred compensation

    o Nontaxable benefits (including health, disability, and life insurance)

    o Compensation reported in prior Form 990 (for backing out deferred compensation paid out in the current year)

- All organizations must disclose

    o Whether the process for determining compensation of the chief executive officer, other officers, or key employees included a review and approval by independent persons, comparability data, and contemporaneous substantiation of the deliberation and decision

    o Whether a copy of the Form 990 was provided to the organization's governing body before it was filed and the process, if any, the organization uses to review the Form 990 o Whether (and if so, how) the organization makes its governing documents, conflict-of-interest policy, and financial statements available to the public

- Organizations providing $150,000 or more in compensation to any employee must

    o Disclose whether it provides specific perquisites to executives

        - In the past, organizations were not required to disclose whether they provided a residence to their chief executive, which made comparability studies more difficult in sectors in which this is a common practice, such as higher education.

        Fringe benefits that must specifically be reported include (Organizations providing any of the following benefits are also required to report whether they follow a written policy regarding payment or reimbursement of these expenses, and whether they require substantiation prior to reimbursement.) the following:

        - First-class or charter travel

            o Travel for companions

            o Tax indemnification and gross-up payments

            o Discretionary spending amount

            o Payments for business use of personal residence

            o Health or social club dues or initiation fees

            o Personal services (e.g., maid, chauffeur, chef)

- Report if persons making over $150,000:

    o Received a severance payment or change of control payment

    o Participated in, or received payment from, a supplemental nonqualified retirement plan

    o Participated in, or received payment from, an equity-based compensation arrangement

    o If yes to any of the above, the organization must list the persons and amounts.

    o Received or accrued any compensation contingent on the revenues or net earnings of the organization or any related organization

    o Received any other non-fixed payments

- Describe in detail the process used for establishing the compensation the chief executive. In particular, the organization must indicate whether it used any of the following:

    o Compensation committee

    o Independent compensation consultant

    o Form 990 of other organizations

    o Written employment contract

    o Compensation survey or study

    o Approval by the board or compensation committee

Source: Internal Revenue Service, *Instructions for Form 990 2008,* (www.irs.gov/pub/irs-pdf/i990.pdf)

APPENDIX II
FAQs

GENERAL TOPICS

Q: What are the trends toward making nonprofit salaries competitive?

A: Nonprofit salaries rose steadily through 2008, and at least among larger and more complex nonprofits, the gap in salary compensation between for-profits and nonprofits narrowed. Moreover, some pay practices, such as bonus and deferred compensation, formerly seen only in for-profit organizations, have become increasingly common in nonprofit organizations.

That said, nonprofit total compensation still lags behind for-profit pay for positions of the same impact and complexity, and probably always will. In part this is because nonprofits cannot offer equity or other lucrative forms of long-term compensation. The larger reason, however, is that external scrutiny, federal and state oversight, and the internal culture of nonprofits generally discourage the payment of very high levels of compensation. For many nonprofits, financial considerations are also significant limits on executive pay.

The bottom line: Many nonprofits are now appropriately competitive — paying enough to ensure they can hire the talent they need, but not so much that they risk violating the public trust that expects them to focus on their main responsibility, their mission.

Q: How should nonprofits adjust compensation in periods of economic stress?

A: The most important consideration in adjusting compensation is always the financial health of the organization. In a period of financial stress — whether specific to the organization or economy-wide — a nonprofit board should look first at what it can afford, and then at the market. Over time, of course, it can be difficult to hold compensation substantially below market, but boards should not fear holding down pay when times are bad. Indeed, a serious and committed chief executive should take the lead in restraining his or her pay in difficult times. An economy-wide downturn will also mean less pressure to increase compensation, since everyone's pay will be constrained.

What form adjustments should take will depend both on the organization's own circumstances and overall trends. Reactions during the 2008/09 period included reductions in planned increases, pay freezes, and even pay cuts — in almost all cases with the chief executive leading by example and taking a bigger hit than others in the organization.

Q: **What are the similarities and differences between compensation issues faced by nonprofit and for-profit organizations?**

A: Both for-profits and nonprofits face the challenge of balancing the market for executive talent against their internal resources. Nonprofits increasingly are able to use many of the same tools as for-profits in paying their executives. They can use bonus and incentive pay if they wish, and are able to offer some forms of deferred compensation. As a result, base salaries have risen in recent years.

Nevertheless, nonprofits continue to operate under stricter constraints than for-profit organizations. As a result, total compensation at nonprofits remains generally below for-profit levels. Nonprofits face stronger public scrutiny and special legal oversight, through the IRS intermediate sanctions rules and other legal limits on compensation. Nonprofits cannot offer some of the most lucrative features of for-profit compensation, such as equity. Deferred compensation is subject to different, and stricter, rules for nonprofits. Bonus plans are less common, and when they exist, generally not as rich. Many nonprofits are also restrained in their pay practices by their mission, their culture, and donor and community expectations.

Q: **How do nonprofits determine salaries for chief executives?**

A: This book lays out a step-by-step process for determining chief executive pay. Those steps include

- Reviewing, and if necessary revising, the chief executive title and job description

- Reviewing organizational strategy and objectives and understanding how they connect with chief executive objectives and compensation

- Developing a compensation philosophy to guide decision making

- Understanding and researching the appropriate marketplace

- Understanding and complying with legal requirements

- Understanding and meeting the test of public scrutiny

- Choosing the appropriate level and mix of compensation, including base pay, extra cash compensation (such as bonuses and incentives), deferred compensation, and benefits and perquisites

- Documenting the compensation process and decision

Q: **How does budget size relate to the chief executive's salary?**

A: Budget size and chief executive pay correlate to some degree, and budget size is one of the factors that should be looked at as part of any market analysis. Budget size is also a factor that should be reviewed as part of any intermediate sanctions analysis.

That said, budget size by no means perfectly correlates with chief executive pay. Staff size, location, mission, the needs of the organization, its history and culture, and the qualifications and record of chief executive candidates can all affect chief executive pay in ways that swamp the budget size connection.

BOARD RESPONSIBILITY

Q: Should the entire board be aware of and/or approve the chief executive's salary and benefits each year?

A: The entire board should review and approve the chief executive's salary and benefits. The board may delegate responsibility for producing recommendations and the data to back them up to a smaller group or committee of board members. The board may choose to seek advice from an outside expert when considering in detail and approving the chief executive salary and benefits. However, the final compensation package should be approved by the board as a whole. There is one caveat: Only independent board members (i.e., those whose compensation or employment are not subject to the chief executive, or stand to otherwise benefit from approving the chief executive's compensation) should be involved in the final approval process.

There are several reasons why it is imperative for the full board to review and approve the final compensation package. The board should be comfortable that the compensation package complies with the intermediate sanctions regulations. Nonprofit chief executive compensation is also public information, which must be reported on the organization's IRS Form 990. All board members should consider the public scrutiny that may be generated by the compensation package, and fully prepared to justify the package. There is now an additional reason for the board to consider public reaction to the decision on chief executive compensation: The new IRS Form 990 asks whether the Form 990 has been shared with the board. A board that does not review the 990 (including the chief executive compensation, which must be appear on it) may raise questions about the effectiveness of the organization's governance process.

Q: Our board has not historically approved the chief executive's salary and benefit package. We currently do not know specifics, so we need to get that information. Is it acceptable to ask the chief executive to give us his salary, cost of health insurance, pension, and other information?

A: It is not just acceptable, it is essential that you know your chief executive's compensation. There should be a formal board process for receiving information about executive compensation, and with today's legal and public scrutiny, compensation information is best shared with the entire board. The board, either in its entirety or through a delegated committee, is responsible for setting chief executive pay. We strongly recommend that the full board make the final decision on pay; it is strongly encouraged by the IRS to review compensation in detail. The board cannot do its job without knowing the full details of chief executive compensation. Staff must provide this information on request — usually through the already established board governance process.

Q: **Can the board limit what it is willing to pay for a chief executive position and indicate that certain benefits are not negotiable?**

A: Yes. The board is responsible for setting chief executive compensation, and for setting limits on what it will pay, or what benefits it will or will not consider. Of course, the board must also accept that its position may mean it cannot hire certain candidates.

LEGAL ISSUES

Q: **Which laws should the board be familiar with when setting the chief executive's compensation?**

A: Board members need to be familiar with the IRS intermediate sanctions rules and related legal doctrines, such as the private inurement doctrine. They also need to understand the state law applying to their nonprofit. If the board considers deferred compensation arrangements, it needs to understand the federal tax law governing such arrangements. See our discussion of legal issues in Chapters 6 and 8.

Q: **What is the IRS text on intermediate sanctions?**

A: The intermediate sanctions rules are included in Internal Revenue Code Section 4958. The Internal Revenue Service Instructions for Form 990 includes an informative discussion of the intermediate sanctions regulations. (See www.irs.gov/instructions/ for more information.)

Q: **Are 501(c)(6) organizations included in intermediate sanctions?**

A: Intermediate sanctions apply only to 501(c)(3) and 501(c)(4) organizations. Internal Revenue Code Section 4958 details the application of the intermediate sanctions rules. Other types of tax-exempt organizations, including 501(c)(6) organizations, are covered by the closely-related private inurement doctrine, which also prohibits excessive compensation. See Chapter 6 for a further discussion of intermediate sanctions and related doctrine. We recommend that all nonprofits follow the intermediate sanctions standards, even if they are not formally covered; this is likely to provide some protection from the IRS.

Q: **Are chief executive pay records public information? What about the pay of other employees?**

A: Chief executive pay, including cash pay and benefits, must be reported on the annual IRS Form 990 that almost all tax-exempt organizations must file. Organizations must also report on their 990s compensation for: a) officers, directors, and trustees; b) "key employees" (the top 20 employees who receive at least $150,000 in reportable income and have fiscal or program management responsibility for at least 10 percent of the organization's financial resources); and c) the top five employees not included in (a) or (b) who receive at least $100,000 in reportable compensation. IRS Form 990s must be made available to the public upon request.

OVERALL COMPENSATION

Q: How much money should a chief executive make? Should it exceed the combined salaries of the rest of the employees?

A: There is no single answer to how much money a chief executive should make. Chief executive pay should be consistent with that of the appropriate marketplace (as the IRS guidelines implementing the intermediate sanctions rules put it, the pay should be set at the "value that would ordinarily be paid for like services by like enterprises under like circumstances"). This book explains in detail how to determine an appropriate market salary for a chief executive. Boards also, of course, need to review the financial circumstances of the organization; it is impossible to pay at the market if the organization cannot afford it.

As for the chief executive's pay relative to that of other employees, as a general rule chief executive pay is 60 percent to 70 percent above that of the next highest paid employee. It would therefore be unusual to see chief executive pay higher than the combined salaries of other employees, and so large a differential might have an impact on employee morale. But without knowing the market for the chief executive and the duties of the other employees, we cannot give a definitive answer to this question.

Q: Can you give me a list of the common compensation surveys?

A: A list of representative national surveys, as well as some regional and specialized surveys, is included in the Suggested Resources at the end of this book. Each organization should also look carefully for local and regional survey data, and for survey information for organizations of its type. Such information may be available from an association representing similar nonprofits.

PERFORMANCE EVALUATION AND INCENTIVE-BASED COMPENSATION

Q: We are in the process of evaluating our chief executive's performance. How do we link this to compensation?

A: We recommend an annual chief executive performance review tied to the board governance process. The best way to link compensation to performance is to decide before the evaluation the rewards associated with achieving your organization's objectives. Thus, you could agree with the chief executive that achieving stated objectives would mean (finances allowing) a certain percentage increase in salary, or the award of an incentive amount, or some combination of the two. Going beyond the objectives would be worth more.

We also recommend that objectives be set in three categories: strategic objectives (the Harvard Balanced Scorecard approach is useful for deciding on strategic objectives), performance against unanticipated challenges, and leadership. Objectives may be given different weightings (i.e., be worth a different percentage of the overall assessment) based on their importance to the organization. Measures for achieving success should be as concrete as possible.

In the absence of an existing link between pay and performance, the next best thing is to decide on an appropriate reward (a salary increase, an ad hoc bonus, or some combination of the two) and carefully explain to the chief executive the particular achievements that justify the boost in pay. That explanation could then serve as the basis for the following year's performance plan.

Remember that any bonus or salary increase must not increase compensation by so much that it creates intermediate sanctions concerns.

Q: Is incentive-based compensation for the chief executive of a nonprofit legal?

A: Yes, incentive-based compensation for the chief executive of a nonprofit is legal, and it is an increasingly common practice among nonprofits. Many nonprofits find incentives an effective way to link chief executive pay to organizational performance and objectives. The total amount of compensation, including the incentive, must be consistent with market practice, however, to meet the intermediate sanctions and related legal standards.

Q: My board chair and I would like to know what is common practice, or what options exist, for building in merit raises/bonuses for chief executive contracts. How do other nonprofits handle this? Is it put in the contract? Is it tied to performance?

A: It is not uncommon for chief executive contracts to include guidelines for merit raises and/or bonuses. The contracts will generally either provide a mechanism for adjusting pay or provide for regular increases or bonuses at board discretion. Pay might, for example, increase annually by the salary movement in your area as reported by an authoritative survey source. Incentives could be linked to the achievement of certain objectives, or to the chief executive's remaining on the job for a certain number of years.

Even when the mechanism for adjusting salaries and providing bonuses is included in a contract, the board usually retains some discretion in adjusting the amount awarded on the basis of performance and/or the organization's financial status. We believe it is important for boards to be able to adjust compensation to reflect performance and the financial condition of the organization, and strongly recommend that adjustments not be completely automatic. Contracts with incentives will often specify the incentive amount but leave it to the board to establish organizational goals and assess the chief executive on the attainment of those goals.

We recommend that performance be awarded annually through a formal board review which includes preset performance objectives. Salary should be adjusted based on inflation/market movement and performance. Any incentive earned should be awarded will based on performance.

Please see the discussion page 93 for best practices on designing a performance management system to decide merit increases and incentive plans.

Q: Is it common, or ethical, for the chief executive to receive incentive compensation based on fundraising revenues?

A: Revenue-based incentives are not common and are considered unethical by many nonprofits. The Association of Fundraising Professionals prohibits its members from receiving such compensation, and states that, where such compensation is percentage-based, "charitable mission can become secondary to self-gain" and "there is incentive for self-dealing to prevail over donors' best interests."[55] Donors may also feel such arrangements are unethical; therefore, organizations should be very cautious in linking fundraising to compensation. One way to avoid any possible appearance of unethical behavior is by having an organizational size objective rather than an explicit fundraising objective. It is also good practice to make financial goals only one of several objectives; see the discussion in Chapter 2 on the balanced scorecard approach to objective setting.

From a legal standpoint, compensation arrangements that are at least in part based on the revenues of the organization are permissible under intermediate sanctions so long as their total amount is reasonable. Nevertheless, such arrangements are a red flag for intermediate sanctions purposes: The fact that they may lead to exceptionally large awards means that they may trigger special scrutiny from the IRS. Therefore, boards should consider the maximum amount that might be earned under such arrangements. The authors strongly recommend including a cap on compensation under such arrangements in order to ensure compliance with the law.

Q: What is a legal cap on executive compensation?

A: The legal cap, as laid out in the intermediate sanctions rules and related legal doctrines, is that "excess" compensation cannot be paid — i.e., more than is justified by the benefit the executive brings to the organization and by the compensation practices of "like organizations" in the marketplace. This text explains in detail how to determine excessive compensation under intermediate sanctions.

BENEFITS

Q: I think our chief executive receives too many benefits. How can I determine the appropriate level?

A: From a legal perspective, the key issue is the amount of total compensation, which means base pay plus any incentives and benefits. That amount should be compared to the market, as explained in Chapter 5. Assuming the total amount of pay is reasonable when compared with the market, your next step would be to review standard survey data, which will typically include information on the prevalence of particular benefits. A review of such data can help you decide if your organization's practices are out of line with the market. Ultimately, however, the decision on what is appropriate will require weighing the cost of the benefits and other payments that your organization makes to the chief executive against the chief executive's value to the organization.

[55] Association of Fundraising Professionals, "Position Paper: Percentage-Based Compensation," www.Afpnet.org/tier3_cd.cfm?folder_id=899&content_itemid=1227 (accessed February 11, 2005).

Q: Do nonprofits offer sabbaticals?

A: While sabbaticals are not a common benefit among nonprofits in general, some nonprofits, especially in the educational and religious sectors, do offer them.

Q: Our organization provides an automobile for the chief executive, which she is able to use for her private needs as well. Is this acceptable?

A: A nonprofit organization may provide an automobile for the chief executive, and the benefit is a reasonably common one, especially among larger nonprofits or when the automobile is necessary for fulfilling the job requirements. However, there should be a clear benefit to the organization for providing the automobile. Otherwise, the perk is likely to appear to the public as an unnecessary luxury. Personal use of the vehicle is taxable income to the chief executive.

Q: Should we provide a small mortgage to our chief executive?

A: Housing assistance is a relatively uncommon, although not unknown, benefit among nonprofits. A number of colleges and universities, for example, provide housing to their chief executives, with the expectation that the residence will be used frequently to entertain potential donors.

Some nonprofits also provide low-interest or no-interest loans to their chief executives. Such loans do not constitute an excess benefit transaction per se, since the chief executive must repay the loan. The interest subsidy (i.e., the amount by which the interest rate falls below fair market value), however, is private compensation and must be taken into account in determining the reasonableness of compensation for legal purposes. The interest subsidy may also be a taxable benefit to the chief executive. Some states (for example, the District of Columbia) prohibit loans to nonprofit officers and directors. The size and creditworthiness of the borrower should also be taken into account. A loan that represents a large portion of the organization's assets, for example, may violate the private inurement doctrine. From a public perception standpoint, any loan should be justifiable in terms of its benefit to the organization.

Q: Do you have any statistics on severance pay agreements?

A: Severance pay is a fairly common benefit among nonprofit organizations. About 41 percent of organizations in one recent survey of national nonprofits provided severance packages.[56] In our experience, median severance is one year at the chief executive level.

---

[56] PRM Consulting, *2008 Management Compensation Report: Not-for-Profit Organizations.*

Q: Are signing bonuses frowned upon by donors, the IRS, or others? Can we hire someone at $65,000 per year and give him or her half up front and the rest later as regular pay?

A: Sign-on bonuses are quite rare in the nonprofit world, but they are not unknown. As long as the total amount of compensation is not excessive, there should be no IRS concerns; moreover, if this is genuinely an arm's-length initial contract, it should be subject to the initial contract exception to the intermediate sanctions regulations. The authors know of no ethical bar to the suggested arrangement.

CONTRACTING

Q: What are the advantages/disadvantages of chief executive employment contracts? How common is the practice? What should be included? What should be the duration?

A: Organizations should draft a formal employment contract in all but the simplest employment relationships. A formal contract provides security to both the executive and to the board, and makes absolutely clear the details of the compensation arrangement and the mutual expectations of the two parties. The employment contract also offers some added security to both the executive and the organization by demonstrating the organization's commitment to the executive. In our experience, a formal contract is increasingly common.

The most important elements of a chief executive contract are listed in Chapter 8. A typical contract duration is three to five years; three years is most common in our experience.

Q: Do chief executives negotiate?

A: Of course they do. Boards need to negotiate, too. The authors hope that this book will help boards understand how to discover the appropriate pay and benefits for their organizations, and so give them the tools they need to negotiate effectively.

APPENDIX III
SAMPLE COMPENSATION COMMITTEE CHARTER

PURPOSE:

The purpose of the Compensation Committee (the "Committee") is to aid the board of Directors (the "board") in discharging its responsibilities relating to compensation of the staff of Organization XYZ.

RESPONSIBILITIES:

The Committee's responsibilities include

- Determination of the compensation philosophy for the Organization, updated as necessary to reflect any changes in the law or the organization's operations

- Negotiation and approval of the chief executive's contract

- Annual review of the chief executive's performance in light of the Organization's goals and objectives

- Recommendation to the full board on the chief executive's compensation level, structure, and adjustment process

- Regular review of compensation for executives and other positions considered "disqualified persons" under IRS intermediate sanctions (including the chief executive):

  o The chief executive will have sole authority for setting the compensation for all employees other than himself or herself. However, the Committee will regularly review compensation for all executives and employees who are considered "disqualified persons" (including the chief executive), to ensure that their compensation complies with

    - the organization's compensation philosophy

    - the rules governing tax-exempt organizations described in the Internal Revenue Code, including, but not limited to, the intermediate sanctions statute (Section 4958) and regulations.

    - the compensation rules and regulations promulgated by any other regulatory agency or legislative authority

- The review will include base salary, bonus payments (if any), deferred compensation payments, retirement arrangements, fringe benefits, severance agreements, employment agreements, and any form of compensation promised therein, and any other compensation items.

- The review will obtain and rely on relevant data on practices at comparable organizations.

- In the case of the chief executive, the Committee will base its recommendation on compensation upon this review.

- Regularly review the organization's compensation structure to ensure that it complies with the compensation philosophy

- Regularly review the organization's bonus/incentive program and determine the size of the bonus/incentive pool, based on performance against strategic milestones or other relevant performance factors determined by the board

- The Committee will make a formal report to the full board on the results of all reviews, including review of compensation for executives who are "disqualified persons" (including the chief executive), review of the compensation structure for compliance with the compensation philosophy, and review of the bonus/incentive program.

AUTHORITY:

The Committee will make recommendations to the full board regarding all plans designed and intended to provide compensation for the chief executive and for such other senior executives who are deemed to be "disqualified persons" under Section 4958, as well as recommendations resulting from review of any other issue for which the Committee has been designated as the supervisory body.

- The full board will have ultimate decision-making authority on any issue for which the Committee has oversight. Final approval of the chief executive's contract and compensation may only be determined by a vote of the board.

- The Committee will have authority to engage outside independent compensation, accounting, legal, and other advisors and to obtain advice and assistance from such independent advisors.

- The Committee will review data from studies prepared by an independent third party to assist in the evaluation of senior executive compensation.

MEMBERSHIP:

- The Committee will consist of no fewer than ____ [at least 3] board members who are independent and who have not been employed by Organization XYZ in the last five years.

- There will be a Chair of the Committee, who will be appointed by the board Chair, with approval of the board.

- No member of the Committee may be an executive, related to an executive, be in a position to benefit from any executive's compensation arrangement, or otherwise have a conflict of interest.

- No member of the Committee may have any other conflict of interest, as determined by board's general conflict-of-interest policy.

- No member of the Committee may be in a position to receive compensation or other economic benefits from any executive or from any transaction arrangement that is subject to the approval of any executive.

MEETINGS:

The Committee will meet at least ___ times annually. The Committee may meet via teleconference. Special meetings of the Committee may also be called by the Chair of the Committee. The attendance of ___ [at least 3] Committee members, whether in person or by teleconference, will constitute a quorum for these meetings.

The Committee will keep written minutes of each of its meetings and will duly file the minutes with the archives of board minutes. Reports of meetings of the Committee will be made to the board at the board's next regularly scheduled meeting following the Committee meeting and will be accompanied by any recommendations to the board approved by the Committee.

APPENDIX IV
SAMPLE CHIEF EXECUTIVE JOB DESCRIPTION

Position Summary: The Chief Executive Officer/President will achieve the organization's mission through implementation of the strategic objectives determined by the organization's Board of Directors (the Board). The chief executive will lead the organization toward advancing its mission by creating new possibilities for project initiatives and grants, fostering innovation, leveraging resources, and establishing partnerships.

The chief executive will manage all operations and activities, including providing direction to the staff and ensuring proper fiscal and operational management.

Reporting: The chief executive reports to the Board. All other staff report to the chief executive.

Duties and Responsibilities:

Strategic

- Work with the Board in its regular strategic planning process and annual review of the strategic plan

- Develop an annual implementation plan with Board review and input

- Provide vision and strategic insight to the Board for fulfilling the mission of the organization, utilizing input from multiple sources, including all staff members

- Direct priorities for program activities in a manner that is consistent with the strategic plan and intent of the Board

- Identify new opportunities to leverage resources in an effort to maximize impact

- Attend meetings, conferences, and review literature to maintain current knowledge of the thinking, issues, and people influencing issues important to the organization's mission

- Assess accomplishments and review failures, and report on those to the Board to inform future thinking and actions

Administrative

- Set the operational policies for the organization, and oversee their proper execution

- Assemble and manage the organization's staff; ensure that the organization attracts and retains the talent necessary to successfully carry out its programs and mission; hire and fire staff members as necessary

- Establish compensation policy and levels consistent with review of overall compensation budget and philosophy by Board

- Develop necessary organizational processes and structures

- Ensure that the organization operates within the financial parameters set by the Board, and that available resources are distributed appropriately

- Provide fiscal oversight for the organization's investments, budgets, and financial reporting

- Propose annual budgets for the organization's operations and programmatic activities

- Monitor monthly financial transactions

- Report regularly to the Board on financial status

Program Activities

- Ensure that current programs are consistent with mission and identify new programs and methods to accomplish the organization's mission

- Ensure that programs and services meet the expectations of the Board and other stakeholders

- Provide oversight and guidance on the development of new programs and program areas

- Maintain current knowledge in select areas

- Convene and lead staff discussions regarding strategic, operational, and tactical issues

Representation

- Advance the mission and image of the organization by serving as the chief representative of the organization to all stakeholders, including the Board, staff, donors and/or members, the media, the government, and the general public

- Develop the organization's communication strategy for external positioning

- Design and, when appropriate, develop (or review) reports, publications, presentations, articles, and other communications (including Web-based and other new media) to disseminate and promote the organization's activities

Development

- Lead organization fundraising activities

- Identify and develop new sources for revenue (increased membership/services/donors)

Board Responsibilities

- Report regularly to the Board on the activities of the organization and progress toward meeting strategic objectives

- Ensure that Board members are kept informed of matters and developments that warrant their attention

- Ensure that Board members are kept up-to-date on best practices on organizational management and leadership

- Identify issues and policies that require the action of the Board

- Assist the Board in the development of strategic objectives

- Work with the Chair to structure and guide Board meetings allowing opportunity for discussion and input

Other

- Perform other duties as assigned

Qualifications: The chief executive will have extensive experience in the management of organizations of comparable size and mission, and possess sufficient expertise on issues relevant to the organization to make well-informed mission-related decisions and command the confidence and respect of stakeholders necessary to serve as the leader of the organization.

Will typically have a minimum of 15-20 years of leadership experience; an advanced degree or equivalent experience; plus strong planning, interpersonal, communications and networking skills.

APPENDIX V
SAMPLE CHIEF EXECUTIVE CONTRACT

Readers are encouraged to use this contract as an example only, to gain insight and guidance. Individual boards and organizations should create a contract according to the specific circumstances they are facing, and in doing so, should seek legal advice and review for any written agreement.

This Agreement is made between the ABC NONPROFIT (ABC) and NONPROFIT EXECUTIVE (Executive), for mutual consideration, the receipt and adequacy of which is acknowledged by the parties, who agree:

1. **Term.** Executive is engaged by the ABC Board of Directors to serve as Executive Director of ABC for a three (3) year period from January 1, 20XX to December 31, 20XX (subject to the terms of paragraph 6 below). This contract, if mutually agreed by ABC and Executive in their sole discretion, may by December 31, 20XX be extended for an additional one (1) year period following successful completion of and positive performance reviews during both of the first two years of the contract. Provided that positive performance reviews continue in subsequent years, the contract, if then mutually agreed by ABC and Executive in their sole discretion, may be extended for one additional year following each positive performance year and, if so agreed, a contract with a term of two (2) years would exist at the commencement of each calendar year (subject to the terms of paragraph 6 below).

2. **Duties.**

   a. Executive will exert his full time and energy to his duties as the Executive Director of ABC. His duties and responsibilities as Executive Director are as customarily performed by a person in such position and as specified in ABC's bylaws, any position description for Executive Director, ABC's rules, policies and other governing documents, by ABC's Board of Directors, and by this Agreement. Executive is the chief employed officer who shall act at all times with a fiduciary duty to ABC. Executive reports to the Board of Directors and on a day-to-day basis the chair of ABC acts as the direct contact for any concerns.

   b. Executive shall work in the (City X) area as designated by ABC.

   c. Executive shall be responsible for developing and recommending to ABC's Board of Directors the annual budget and staffing plans. Executive shall have the authority to hire, supervise, evaluate, and terminate all ABC employees based on the approved staffing plan.

3. **Performance Evaluation.** Evaluation and assessment of the performance of Executive shall be conducted on an ongoing basis by the ABC President and ABC's officers, resulting in a formal written evaluation at least annually, prior to the anniversary date of this Agreement. The evaluation shall be based on an annual performance plan to be mutually developed by Executive and ABC's President and officers. The annual performance plan shall provide for and assess performance of the general management of ABC and measurable goals and objectives for ABC and the Executive Director, taking into account the financial and staff resources made available by ABC. The annual performance plan shall be completed no later than the third month following the anniversary date of this Agreement. In the event that Executive's performance is found to be unsatisfactory, the ABC President shall describe in writing, in reasonable detail, specific examples of unsatisfactory performance. Upon the conclusion of the annual evaluation, ABC's governing board, in its sole discretion, shall determine the amount or type of increase in the salary and/or benefits of Executive to be made for the upcoming contract year.

4. **Salary and Benefits.**

   a. The base salary of Executive is payable at the annual rate of One-hundred Thousand Dollars ($100,000). After the first year, Executive shall be entitled to an annual cost of living adjustment to base salary based on movement in the nonprofit marketplace, in addition to any merit increases awarded in the sole discretion of ABC.

   b. Executive shall be entitled to the following paid benefits: (i) a contribution to a pension plan acceptable to ABC at a rate equivalent to the annual rate of 10 percent of salary; (ii) annual leave at the rate of 15 days the first year, and at the rate of 20 days for each of the next two (2) years (with no more than two (2) weeks eligible for roll-over and use in any year). A maximum of two (2) weeks annual leave will be compensated at the expiration or termination of this contract; (iii) paid holidays at the rate of eight (8) days per year (on days to be determined by Executive consistent with his duties and responsibilities to ABC); (iv) sick leave at the rate of one (1) day per month, with a maximum of 200 hours of accrued but unused sick leave during the full-term of this contract; (v) personal leave at the rate of three (3) days per year; (vi) bereavement leave at the rate of three (3) days in the event of a death in the immediate family of Executive or his spouse; (vii) health insurance under a preferred provider organization selected by ABC, for single, individual coverage; (viii) life insurance in the amount of two (2) times the salary of Executive; (ix) disability insurance selected by ABC in its sole discretion; provided, however, that no salary or benefits may be taken or accrued until they are earned. The salary and benefits identified in this paragraph 4 constitutes the entire payment and compensation by ABC for the services of Executive.

5. **Business Expenses.** ABC will annually pay or reimburse Executive for reasonable and necessary business expenses up to Ten Thousand Dollars

($10,000) incurred by Executive which are directly related to the performance of his duties of employment, including travel, professional memberships and professional development, subject to documentation by Executive and approval by ABC.

6. **Cancellation and Severance.**

   a. ABC may cancel this Agreement immediately in the event of the death of Executive or the dissolution of ABC.

   b. ABC may cancel this Agreement 12 work weeks plus one day after the onset of physical or mental disability that prevents the effective performance of his duties for 12 work weeks plus one day or more provided that after such cancellation ABC shall then continue to pay Executive's salary either (i) for one-hundred twenty (120) days or (ii) until the date when disability insurance coverage commences, whichever is sooner.

   c. ABC may cancel this Agreement immediately if Executive engages in an act or omission of dishonesty, fraud, misrepresentation, conflict of interest, breach of fiduciary duty, or any act of misfeasance, malfeasance or moral turpitude. Upon cancellation, ABC must disclose to Executive the act or omission upon which the cancellation of this Agreement is based.

   d. ABC may cancel this Agreement for other reasons, with or without cause, which need not be disclosed to Executive, by giving Executive thirty (30) days notice in writing, and then paying to Executive severance consisting of six (6) months salary plus one additional month salary for each year of completed service to ABC up to a total of 12 months, a maximum of two weeks accrued but unused annual leave (but not accrued or other unused sick leave or any other leave), and the dollar value of six (6) months plus one additional month of all other benefits as described in paragraph 4. Payments shall be made on a regular twice-monthly basis during a period equal to six (6) months plus one additional month for each year of completed service to ABC.

   e. Upon the expiration, cancellation or termination of this Agreement with or without cause, no accrued or other unused sick leave shall be compensated.

   f. Executive may cancel this Agreement by giving ABC at least thirty (30) days advance notice in writing.

   g. The content and procedures set forth in this Agreement (and not those set forth in any ABC handbook or manual relating to employees generally) govern this Agreement in general and its cancellation in particular.

7. **Successors.** This Agreement is binding upon ABC and Executive, their heirs, executors, administrators, successors, and assigns. Executive will not assign or delegate any part of his rights or responsibilities under this Agreement unless ABC agrees in writing to the assignment or delegation. In the event of any merger, consolidation or reorganization involving ABC, this Agreement becomes an obligation of any legal successor or successors to ABC.

8. **Indemnification.** ABC shall indemnify, hold harmless, and defend Executive against all claims arising against Executive, his heirs, administrators and/or executors in connection with his employment by ABC and as permitted by law. Executive shall immediately notify the President and legal counsel of ABC orally and in writing upon learning of any actual or threatened dispute or legal process and shall cooperate fully in any defense or action.

9. **Entire Agreement.** This Agreement contains the entire Agreement between ABC and Executive. It may not be changed or renewed orally but only by an Agreement in writing signed by the President upon prior Board of Directors resolution and by Executive. This Agreement supersedes and cancels all previous agreements between ABC and Executive.

10. **Headings not controlling.** The headings of sections of this Agreement are not controlling.

11. **Governing law.** This Agreement is governed by the laws of the [District of Columbia].

Executive   Date

President, ABC   Date

Source: Adapted and reprinted with permission from Pfau Englund Nonprofit Law, P.C. For more information please visit www.nonprofitlaw.com, call 703-304-1204, or e-mail spfau@nonprofitlaw.com.

GLOSSARY

Annual increase/raise — The yearly increase in base salary provided by most organizations, if allowed by their financial condition. Annual increases are generally a combination of a percentage increase reflecting inflation and an additional amount rewarding performance. Some chief executive contracts provide for annual base salary increases. This is done either at the discretion of the board or linked to market movement as reported in compensation surveys or government cost of living indices. Annual increases are also sometimes referred to as merit increases or cost of living increases.

Applicable tax-exempt organization — Intermediate sanctions regulations apply only to Internal Revenue Code 501(c)(3) public charities and 501(c)(4) social welfare organizations. These are called by the IRS applicable tax-exempt organizations. Other tax-exempt organizations are not formally subject to intermediate sanctions. They are, however, still subject to the private inurement doctrine, and a prudent board should act as if intermediate sanctions apply to its organization even if it is not a (c)(3) or (c)(4) by, for example, basing chief executive compensation on documented market practice.

Balanced scorecard approach — The balanced scorecard approach is based on the idea that financial performance measures alone do not necessarily ensure long-term organizational health. The balanced scorecard organizes objectives into four primary areas of performance: customer (or mission in the case of nonprofits), financial, internal, and innovation and learning. The balanced scorecard works especially well with nonprofit organizations as financial performance is not the primary criterion for organizational success.

Bonus — Compensation provided, often at the end of the year, in addition to regular base compensation. A bonus is generally provided as a reward for strong performance. A bonus can be part of a formal performance plan, or can be ad hoc. The terms bonus and incentive are sometimes used synonymously, but incentives are almost always linked to particular objectives, while bonuses may or may not be. Bonuses must be included as part of total compensation for intermediate sanctions purposes.

Conflict of interest — Individuals have a conflict of interest if they are on both sides of an actual or potential transaction. Persons who have a conflict of interest are anyone whose employment is subject to the person whose compensation he or she would approve, or anyone who would otherwise stand to benefit financially from approving the compensation.

Consideration — Consideration is a legal term meaning the bargained-for value exchanged between contracting parties. In the case of an employment contract, the consideration is typically service by the employee and compensation from the employer.

Correction period — The IRS provides for a correction period between the finding of an excess benefit under the intermediate sanctions regulations and the application of the second-tier penalty (the first-tier 25 percent penalty applies in any case). The correction period is, unless extended, 90 days after the date of mailing of a notice of deficiency (IRC § 6212). After the correction period, the second-tier intermediate sanctions penalty applies — an excise tax set at 200 percent of the excess benefit.

Disqualified person — A disqualified person for intermediate sanctions purposes is someone who is in a position to exercise substantial influence with respect to the affairs of an organization subject to the intermediate sanctions regulations, i.e., an applicable tax-exempt organization. Disqualified persons include officers, key employees, board members, close relatives of officers and board members, and others in a position to influence the organization.

Excess benefit — An excess benefit is the economic value of any benefit received by a disqualified person that is in excess of the value he or she provides to the organization [see IRC § 4958(c)(1)(B)]. An example of an excess benefit is the amount of compensation provided to a nonprofit chief executive that is above reasonable market compensation for someone providing "like services by like enterprises under like circumstances."

Excess benefit transaction — For intermediate sanctions purposes, an excess benefit transaction is any transaction on the part of an applicable tax-exempt organization where the value of the benefit provided to a disqualified person is greater than any benefit the organization receives in turn [IRC § 4958(c)(1)(A)].

Fiduciary — A fiduciary is a person responsible for the administration, investment, and distribution of assets belonging to another person, or to an organization. The duties of the fiduciary are termed fiduciary responsibility.

Form 990 — IRS Form 990 is an IRS annual return that almost all tax-exempt organizations must file every year. The information on the form 990 must be made available to the public.

Incentive pay — Incentive pay is compensation paid in addition to base salary in response to the achievement of organizational or individual objectives. These objectives, and the amount to be paid upon the achievement of the objectives are generally specified in advance, often through a formal performance plan. Incentives may take the form of a percentage of a financial gain to the organization such as revenue raised or cost savings achieved. Although the terms are sometimes used interchangeably, incentive pay differs from bonus compensation because it is linked to particular objectives, not to general performance. Incentive pay must be included as part of total compensation for intermediate sanctions purposes.

Independent board — An independent board is one that has no individuals who have a conflict of interest with regard to the person receiving or potentially receiving an economic benefit from the organization.

Initial contract exception — Under the intermediate sanctions regulations, the initial contract exception exempts transactions that are part of the initial relationship between an applicable tax-exempt organization and a disqualified person.

Insider — See disqualified person.

Intermediate sanctions — Intermediate sanctions has come to be used as a shorthand term for the federal regulations barring excess compensation and other excess benefits for officers, key management employees, board members, and other insiders at certain tax-exempt nonprofit organizations. Intermediate sanctions apply only to Internal Revenue Code 501(c)(3) public charities and 501(c)(4) social welfare organizations. In form, intermediate sanctions are federal excise taxes (IRC § 4958), which are imposed on disqualified persons who engage in excess benefit transactions with applicable tax exempt organizations, and on organization managers who knowingly approve of such transactions. The sanctions are termed "intermediate" because they are between IRS inaction and revocation of the organization's tax-exempt status. Other tax-exempt organizations are subject to the private inurement doctrine, which imposes similar restrictions, but without the detailed excise tax and regulatory regime of intermediate sanctions.

Merit increases — A term used to refer to annual salary increases for the employees of an organization. Although termed merit increases, most or all of the annual increase is often a cost of living increase. Organizations do, however, often increase or reduce the amount of the merit increase based on an individual's job performance.

Percentage-based compensation — Percentage-based compensation is compensation that provides for the recipient to get a percentage share of a financial gain, e.g., an amount of revenue raised. Gain-sharing or other percentage-based compensation arrangements, including arrangements based on the revenues of the organization, are permissible under intermediate sanctions so long as their total amount is reasonable. However, there should be proportionate benefit to the organization from such plans. The authors recommend that boards be especially careful in assessing such plans for their consistency with the market.

Perquisites — Benefits provided to a senior official at an organization — a chief executive or board member, for example. Perquisites differ from other benefits in being restricted to the most senior persons in an organization. Generally, they are not a direct financial benefit and many, but not all, are relatively modest in cost. They can include special parking arrangements, provision of housing, club memberships, spouse travel, sabbatical arrangements, and others.

Private foundation — A type of charitable organization, generally characterized as (a) being a charitable entity; (b) often funded from a limited number of sources, such as an individual, a family, or a corporation; (c) operating from investment income rather than contributions; and (d) making grants to other charitable organizations rather than funding and conducting its own program(s).

Private inurement doctrine — Private inurement is the diversion of an organization's assets or income to persons, generally insiders, who have not earned or merited it. Federal tax law differentiates nonprofit organizations from for-profit organizations by forbidding private inurement. Under the doctrine, tax-exempt organizations cannot provide income or assets to persons with a significant relationship with the organization (insiders) for their private purposes, through, for example, unreasonable compensation.

Public charity — A public charity is an IRC § 501(c)(3) organization that receives support from a wide range of sources or meets other specific requirements, such as a church, school, or hospital.

Publicly supported charity — Publicly supported charities are those that are supported through public donations (i.e., donations from a large number of individuals, rather than from a single individual or small number of individuals). This distinguishes them from private foundations.

Rebuttable presumption of reasonableness — The rebuttable presumption of reasonableness is a partial safe harbor under the intermediate sanctions regulations that shifts the burden of proof to the IRS in showing that there has been an excess benefit transaction if certain conditions are met. Three conditions are required for the rebuttable presumption of reasonableness:

1. The compensation arrangement must be approved in advance by an authorized body of the applicable tax-exempt organization, composed entirely of individuals with no conflict of interest with respect to the compensation arrangement.

2. The authorized body obtained and relied on appropriate data as to comparability prior to making determination.

3. An authorized body must adequately document the basis for its determination.

Revenue-sharing arrangement — In a revenue-sharing arrangement, a person receives a payment from a tax-exempt organization based on the organization's income, for example, a commission. Compensation arrangements that are at least in part based on the revenues of the organization are permissible under intermediate sanctions so long as their total amount is reasonable. However, the organization should receive proportionate benefit from such plans. The authors recommend that boards be especially careful in assessing such plans for their consistency with the market.

Salary cap — An upper limit on salaries within an organization. A salary cap may reflect financial constraints, the organization's culture and mission, the wishes of donors and supporters, or a combination of all three. Maintaining a salary cap over time can be difficult if it prevents the organization from recruiting and retaining desired staff. A salary cap can also lead to salary compression if lower level salaries increase with the market and senior salaries do not. This can lead to poor morale and higher turnover among senior staff.

Salary freeze — A salary freeze holds salaries in place throughout an organization. It is generally imposed in times of financial difficulty. Like a salary cap — but even more so — a salary freeze can prevent an organization from recruiting and retaining desired staff. A salary freeze may be unavoidable, however, in times of economic difficulty.

Self-dealing — Self-dealing refers to transactions where someone is in a fiduciary relationship with an organization and acquires or makes use of property that belongs to the organization for his or her own benefit.

Social welfare organization — A social welfare organization is a tax-exempt organization that engages in social welfare, such as civic, activities and is organized under IRC § 501(c)(4).

Tax-exempt organization — A tax-exempt organization is exempt from one or more federal, state, or local taxes, most commonly income tax. IRC § 501(a) and IRC § 501(c)(1)–(27) describe most of the organizations that are exempt from federal income tax.

SUGGESTED RESOURCES
ORGANIZATIONS

The Annie E. Casey Foundation: The foundation offers a series of free monographs on executive transitions. You can find them here: www.aecf.org/KnowledgeCenter/PublicationsSeries/ExecutiveTransitionMonographs.aspx

BoardSource: BoardSource is the premier resource for practical information, tools and best practices, training, and leadership development for board members of nonprofit organizations worldwide. BoardSource, 1828 L Street NW, Suite 900, Washington, DC 20036-5114. 202-452-6262 or 800-883-6262. Fax: 202-452-6299. www.boardsource.org

Chronicle of Higher Education (CHE): CHE regularly publishes articles on compensation trends and issues. It also puts out an annual issue with salary data taken from 990s. The Chronicle of Higher Education, 1255 23rd Street NW, Suite 700, Washington, DC 20037. 202-466-1000. www.chronicle.com

Chronicle of Philanthropy: The *Chronicle of Philanthropy* is a sister publication of the *Chronicle of Higher Education*. The *Chronicle of Philanthropy* is the newspaper of the nonprofit world. It is the news source, in print and online, for charity leaders, fundraisers, grantmakers, and other people involved in the philanthropic enterprise. *Chronicle of Philanthropy,* 1255 23rd Street NW, Suite 700, Washington, DC 20037. 202-466-1000. www.philanthropy.com

College and University Professional Association for Human Resources (CUPA-HR): A good source for information on university practices. Publishes an annual Administrative Compensation Survey. CUPA-HR, Tyson Place, 2607 Kingston Pike, Suite 250, Knoxville, TN 37919. 865-637-7673. Fax: 865-637-7674. www.cupahr.org/surveys/salarysurveysinfo.html

Council on Foundations: A first-rate source for information on foundation practices in general. Publishes an annual Grantmakers Salary Report. Council on Foundations, 1828 L Street NW, Washington, DC 20036. 202-466-6512. Fax: 202-785-3926. www.cof.org

Society for Human Resource Management (SHRM): SHRM is a professional association devoted to human resource management. It provides its members with research, news, educational tools, and information on best practices in all areas of human resource management, including analysis of market data and executive compensation. Society for Human Resources Management, 1800 Duke Street, Alexandria, VA 22314. 800-283-7476. Fax: 703-535-6490. www.shrm.org

WorldatWork: Formerly the American Compensation Association. WorldatWork is a nonprofit professional association for human resources. It provides information on compensation, benefits, and total rewards. Membership is required. WorldatWork, 14040 N. Northsight Blvd., Scottsdale, AZ 85260. 877-951-9191. Fax: 866-816-2962. www.worldatwork.org

GENERAL SURVEY DATA

Abbott, Langer & Associates: Abbot Langer publishes an annual report on Compensation in Nonprofit Organizations. Abbott, Langer & Associates, Inc., Dept. NET, 548 First Street, Crete, IL 60417. 708-672-4200. Fax: 708-672-4674. www.abbott-langer.com

ERI: Economic Resource Institute provides salary survey analyses, geographic differentials, wage surveys, executive compensation information, cost of living comparisons, prevailing wage studies, employee benefit data, and compensation and benefits training. The database provides mostly corporate data but includes numerous positions in the nonprofit world. ERI Economic Research Institute, 8575 164th Avenue NE, Suite 100, Redmond, WA 98052. 800-627-3697. Fax: 800-753-4415. www.erieri.com

GuideStar: An extensive national online database of nonprofit organizations, which provides Form 990 data free of charge. For more detailed analysis a fee is required. GuideStar also publishes an annual Nonprofit Compensation Report. GuideStar, 4801 Courthouse Street, Suite 220, Williamsburg, VA 23188. 757-229-4631. www.guidestar.org

Mercer HR Consulting: Mercer HR provides an annual Benchmark Database Executive Survey Report. The survey is comprised of mostly for-profit data but includes a nonprofit cut. Mercer Human Resource Consulting Inc., 462 South Fourth Street, Suite 1100, Louisville, KY 40202-3415. www.mercerhr.com

PRM Consulting: PRM publishes an annual national Compensation Survey of Management Positions for Not-for-Profit Organizations. PRM Consulting, Inc., 1814 13th Street NW, Washington, DC 20009. 202-745-3700. Fax: 202-745-3701. www.prmconsulting.com

Quatt Associates, Inc./Public Broadcasting Service (PBS): In conjunction with PBS, Quatt Associates, Inc. conducts an annual survey of salary and benefits for major national nonprofit organizations. The survey is available to participants only. Quatt Associates, Inc., 2233 Wisconsin Avenue NW, Suite 501, Washington, DC 20007. 202-342-1000. Fax: 202-338-1000. www.quatt.com

Society for Human Resource Management (SHRM): SHRM is an association devoted to human resource management. It publishes both a Benchmark Compensation Survey and a Benefits Survey annually. Society for Human Resource Management, 1800 Duke Street, Alexandria, VA 22314. 800-283-SHRM (7476). Fax: 703-535-6490. www.shrm.org

Watson Wyatt: Watson Wyatt publishes an annual Top Management Compensation report. This survey includes mostly for-profit data, but a nonprofit cut is provided as well. Watson Wyatt, 1717 H Street NW, Washington, DC 20006. 202-715-7000. Fax: 202-715-7700. www.watsonwyatt.com/research/

REGIONAL SURVEY DATA

A number of regional surveys are available. Examples include the Human Resources Association of the National Capital Area (HRA-NCA) Compensation Survey of the Washington, D.C., metropolitan area (the survey includes both for-profit and nonprofit data, but includes cuts for associations and nonprofits); the Louisiana Nonprofit Salary and Benefit Survey put out by the Louisiana Association of Nonprofit Organizations; and the Colorado Nonprofit Salary & Benefits Survey put out by the Colorado Association of Nonprofits. Visit www.fundsnetservices.com/grantman.htm for a more complete list and contact information.

SURVEYS OF SPECIFIC TYPES OF NONPROFITS

EDUCATION

American Council on Education (ACE): ACE's Publication, The American College President, provides demographic and salary data from all sectors of American higher education. American Council on Education, One Dupont Circle NW, Washington, DC 20036. 202-939-9300. Fax: 202-833-4760. www.acenet.edu

Association of Governing Boards of Universities and Colleges (AGB): One Dupont Circle NW, Suite 400, Washington, DC 20036. 202-296-8400. Fax: 202-223-7053. Membership required. http://data.agb.org/

CUPA-HR: College and University Professional Association for Human Resources. The Association publishes an annual Administrative Compensation Survey. CUPA-HR, Tyson Place, 2607 Kingston Pike, Suite 250, Knoxville, TN 37919. 865-637-7673. Fax: 865-637-7674. www.cupahr.org/surveys/salarysurveysinfo.html

Quatt Associates, Inc./WHES: In conjunction with the Washington Higher Education Secretariat, Quatt Associates conducts an annual survey of salary and benefits of associations in the field of higher education in the Washington, D.C., area. Survey is available to participants only. Quatt Associates, Inc., 2233 Wisconsin Avenue NW, Suite 501, Washington, DC 20007. 202-342-1000. Fax: 202-338-1000. www.quatt.com

Museums

American Association of Museums (AAM): AAM is the resource for compensation issues in the museum field. AAM produces the annual American Association of Museum Directors Salary Survey as well as other surveys on museum compensation and benefits. American Association of Museums, 1575 Eye Street NW, Suite 400, Washington, DC 20005. 202-289-1818. Fax: 202-289-6578. www.aam-us.org

Quatt Associates, Inc.: In conjunction with a consortium of several of the nation's largest museums, Quatt conducts a biennial survey of management and technical and specialty positions in the museum workplace. Survey is available to participants only. Quatt Associates, Inc., 2233 Wisconsin Avenue NW, Suite 501, Washington, DC 20007. 202-342-1000. Fax: 202-338-1000. www.quatt.com

Philanthropic Organizations

Council on Foundations: The Council publishes an annual Grantmakers Salary and Benefits Report. The Council on Foundations, 1828 L Street NW, Washington, DC 20036. 202-466-6512. Fax: 202-785-3926. www.cof.org

New York Regional Association of Grantmakers (NYRAG): NYRAG is a nonprofit membership organization for philanthropy in the NY metropolitan area. NYRAG publishes an annual Compensation Summary of its member organizations. Survey is available to members only. New York Regional Association of Grantmakers, 505 Eighth Avenue, Suite 1805, New York, NY 10018. 212-714-0699. Fax: 212-239-2075. www.nyrag.org

Trade Associations

American Research Company (ARC): ARC publishes an annual National Compensation Study of Association Chief Executives. This is a highly detailed source that focuses exclusively on trade association chief executives. American Research Company, Inc., 10003 Robindale Court, Great Falls, VA 22066. 703-759-3188. Fax: 703-759-3127. www.AmericanReseachCo.com

American Society of Association Executives (ASAE): The Association publishes an annual Executive Compensation and Benefit Survey. American Society of Association Executives, The ASAE Building, 1575 I Street NW, Washington, DC 20005. 888-950-2723 or 202-371-0940. Fax: 202-371-8315. www.asaenet.org

National Journal: The National Journal publishes a biennial survey of association chief executive salaries. The data are taken from Forms 990 or comparable sources. National Journal Group Inc., The Watergate, 600 New Hampshire Avenue NW, Washington, DC 20037. 202-739-8400. Fax: 202-833-8069. 0www.nationaljournal.com

Quatt Associates, Inc./Association Human Resources Group (AHRG): In conjunction with AHRG, Quatt Associates publishes an annual survey of salary and benefits of major national trade organizations. The survey is available to participants only. Quatt Associates, Inc., 2233 Wisconsin Avenue NW, Suite 501, Washington, DC 20007. 202-342-1000. Fax: 202-338-1000. www.quatt.com

PUBLICATIONS

Axelrod, Nancy R. *Chief Executive Succession Planning: The Board's Role in Securing Your Organization's Future.* Washington, DC: BoardSource, 2002. Chief executive succession planning is not only about determining your organization's next leader. It is a continuous process that assesses your organization's needs and identifies leadership that supports those needs. A successful succession plan is linked to your organization's strategic plan, mission, and vision. Author Nancy Axelrod helps board members prepare for the future by examining the ongoing and intermittent steps of executive succession planning.

Barbeito, Carol, and Jack P. Bowman. *Nonprofit Compensation and Benefits Practices.* New York: John Wiley & Sons, 1998. This book provides an overview of current workforce, employment, and compensation trends in the private, government, and nonprofit sectors. In addition, it offers a detailed examination of innovative compensation practices, important guidance on establishing and implementing a competitive compensation plan, and real-world case studies.

Berry, Brian. *Strategic Planning Workbook for Nonprofit Organizations.* St. Paul, MN: Amherst H. Wilder, 1997. Strategic planning is a tool for finding the best future for your organization and the best path to reach that destination. This classic workbook gives you practical guidance through five planning steps. Useful step-by-step worksheets help you develop the plan, involve others in the process, and measure results.

Chait, Richard P., William P. Ryan, and Barbara E. Taylor. *Governance as Leadership: Reframing the Work of Nonprofit Boards.* New York: John Wiley & Sons and Washington, DC: BoardSource, 2005. *Governance as Leadership* introduces a fresh way to think about governance, with sensible guidance to turn these ideas into concrete actions. The book will be particularly valuable to staff of professionally managed nonprofit organizations, and to others, including foundation officers, donors, consultants, and students of nonprofit organizations, who are interested in improving nonprofit governance.

Hopkins, Bruce R. *The Law of Intermediate Sanctions: A Guide for Nonprofits.* New York: John Wiley & Sons, 2003. This comprehensive, easy-to-use guide provides necessary explanations of the constitution and application of intermediate sanctions — fines and legal actions intended to eliminate nonprofit abuse. The text summarizes, analyzes, and explains the federal tax law on intermediate sanctions, addressing such topics as the statute, legislative history, regulations, and court opinions of intermediate sanctions; the influence of law concerning private inurement, private benefit, and private foundation self-dealing; real-world examples of intermediate sanctions in practice; and how nonprofits may seek to avoid excess benefit transactions or adequately document that excess benefit does not occur.

Mintz, Joshua. *Assessment of the Chief Executive: A Tool for Nonprofit Boards.* Washington, DC: BoardSource, 2005. By failing to adequately evaluate the chief executive, many nonprofit boards miss an opportunity to express support for the executive and strengthen his or her performance. Neglect can be costly, resulting in high turnover, mistrust, and ongoing poor performance. This resource provides a comprehensive tool boards can use in the evaluation process. After discussing the benefits of assessment, the user's guide suggests a process and provides a questionnaire that addresses every major area of responsibility. This tool is also available in online format, which guarantees faster and easer compilation of results.

Ober|Kaler, attorneys at law. *The Nonprofit Legal Landscape.* Washington, DC: BoardSource, 2005. Designed for executives and board members, *The Nonprofit Legal Landscape* explains the laws and legal concepts that affect nonprofit organizations. It serves as a handy reference tool for laws specific to tax exemption and for those regulating general business practices. When confronted with legal questions, nonprofit leaders can use this easy-to-read resource to rise rapidly to the next level of understanding.

Samuels, David G., and Howard Pianko. *Nonprofit Compensation, Benefits, and Employment Law.* New York: John Wiley & Sons, 1998. This reference book covers a broad range of employee-related issues confronting officers, directors, managers, and attorneys of nonprofit organizations. It provides an overview of such topics as intermediate sanctions, IRS audits, nonqualified arrangements, and the Age Discrimination in Employment Act. Also included are a discussion of church plans, a look at employee benefit aspects of mergers and acquisitions, and case studies.

Tebbe, Don. *Chief Executive Transitions: How to Hire and Support a Nonprofit CEO.* Washington, DC: BoardSource, 2009. When a nonprofit finds itself in need of a new chief executive, managing the transition effectively is crucial to the organization's future impact and continued success. This award-winning book will not only help boards navigate the hiring process, but also oversee a successful leadership transition.

ABOUT THE AUTHORS
CHARLES W. QUATT, PH.D.

Charles Quatt is president and founder of Quatt Associates, Inc. Mr. Quatt specializes in compensation, organizational development, performance management systems, and strategic planning.

In addition to his consulting practice, Mr. Quatt has conducted seminars and instructed at American University, Georgetown University, Marymount University, the University of Maryland, and Virginia Tech Business School.

Before establishing Quatt Associates, Mr. Quatt served for almost 10 years as a director of management consulting and practice leader for the Hay Group, an international management consulting firm. Mr. Quatt specialized in compensation, employee opinion surveys, performance management, and organizational development. His clients included Fortune 500 companies as well as a number of nonprofit and government organizations.

Mr. Quatt also worked as a human resources manager for General Electric Company and for Mobil Corporation. At both Mobil Corporation and General Electric Company, his responsibilities included organization development, compensation, performance management, survey research, and employee relations.

Prior to his corporate engagements, Mr. Quatt served as a faculty member for six years at Harvard and Princeton universities. He earned his Ph.D. from Harvard University, where he was a Lehman Scholar. Mr. Quatt serves on the board of the International Center for Research on Women.

BRIAN H. VOGEL

Brian Vogel is a senior principal with Quatt Associates. Mr. Vogel has broad experience in nonprofit compensation, strategic planning, organization development, performance management, and research. His practice has focused on advocacy organizations, foundations, trade and professional associations, and nonprofit media organizations. He leads the firm's intermediate sanctions practice. Prior to joining Quatt Associates, Mr. Vogel was the vice president and managing partner of Policy Services, Inc., a Washington-based consulting firm, specializing in trade association policy and economic analysis. Mr. Vogel also served for 19 years in several policy and government relations positions with the Association of American Railroads, finishing as assistant vice president for policy.

Mr. Vogel is a graduate of Harvard Law School and a graduate of Harvard College. Mr. Vogel serves on the board of Opera Lafayette, a Washington D.C.-based arts organization.